Running Amach in Ireland

RUNNING AMACH IN IRELAND

True Stories by LGBTQ Women

Edited by
Maureen Looney

ORPEN PRESS

Published by
Orpen Press
13 Adelaide Road
Dublin 2
Ireland

email: info@orpenpress.com
www.orpenpress.com

Paperback ISBN 978-1-909895-89-8
ePub ISBN 978-1-909895-91-1
Kindle ISBN 978-1-909895-92-8
PDF ISBN 978-1-909895-93-5

Printed in Dublin by SPRINTprint Ltd.

A candle loses nothing when lighting another candle.

Contents

Preface

In January 2010, I set up Running Amach ('amach' means 'out' in Irish) after realising that there was a serious lack of social outlets for LGBTQ (lesbian, gay, bisexual, transgender and questioning) women in Ireland. Running Amach is an online social networking club using the MeetUp website platform. We 'use the internet to get off the internet'. Running Amach is a collective community and its success is down to the 80+ Event Hosts who have organised thousands of social events for our members.

I began to meet many LGBTQ women from all over Ireland at our social events and I heard so many inspiring, challenging, sad, funny and sometimes unbelievable life stories about being LGBTQ in Ireland. Many of these stories were about the difficult and painful journey of 'coming out'. I started thinking about how supportive such personal recollections would be for women coming out in the future. I was also aware that LGBTQ women in Ireland have been relatively invisible until very recently. So, I encouraged, cajoled, sweet-talked, begged, hounded and flattered Running Amach members into sitting down to write their stories. I gathered 34 stories in the end. The stories are moving, emotional, therapeutic and cathartic. They give a picture of what it was like to be LGBTQ during a time when not many women were out. In essence, this book is making invisible women visible and will be an historical record of our narratives and experiences during a time of taboos, secrets, isolation, exclusion and fear. I am thrilled that

Preface

this book is being published in the year that marriage equality rights were secured for our community in Ireland. We could not have accomplished this without our 'straight alliance' friends and family. Thank you Fairy much!

I wish to thank all the women who submitted stories. It is a brave thing to do. Some of the authors do not use their full name or their real name as they are not fully out. Thanks to Nikki Newman for her design contribution to the book cover. Thanks to Conor Kostick for his advice with the publishing contract. Special thanks to Clodagh Ní Ghallachóir for her encouragement and support with my editing process. Thank you to Ailbhe O'Reilly, Eileen O'Brien and Fiona Dunne in Orpen Press, and also Jennifer Thompson, for their warmth, guidance and professionalism.

Personally, I wish to thank my friends, work colleagues and family in Ireland and Canada for supporting me with this endeavour.

My primary vision for the book is that other women will find it a support for themselves during their coming-out journey, as they discover the truth about themselves. We all have our own story ... but we share many of the same feelings.

Maureen Looney
Founder of Running Amach
http://www.meetup.com/Dublin-LGBTQ-Womens-Social-Networking-Club/

A Date to Remember

When life gets a bit complicated, I find that I sometimes get an unexpected answer, even in the most unusual ways. In this instance, it was a split-second encounter which, quite literally, brought me back to my senses.

I was going through a difficult time emotionally, having had my heart broken once again. One day, as I was walking through central Dublin, I tried to make sense of my situation. Would it be easier to accept that maybe I was supposed to be single? Forget about my desires; forget about ever being intimate with another woman? I was deeply engrossed in my thoughts as I walked through the Irish Film Institute. They were in the middle of a refurbishment, and one area was blocked off with a temporary wall made of fresh-smelling wood. As I passed by, this strong smell brought me right back to an encounter I had had decades before.

It was a rainy day in July. I was a young student in Germany, and it was the end of the academic year. The student union had organised a film screening as a welcome distraction from preparing for our last exams. That's how I ended up in a windowless, airless lecture room, sitting next to another female student. We had both arrived a few minutes before the film was supposed to begin, and we struck up a conversation.

I'd been with my boyfriend for four years by then, but I knew that I was also attracted to women, though I hadn't really done anything about it. Although we sometimes spoke about it, my feelings for women seemed to puzzle me more than him. He found the idea of a threesome with two women quite exciting. However, I never told him that in my fantasies regarding women, three, with only two-thirds being female, didn't really add up for me.

The woman next to me introduced herself as Marion. She was in her mid-twenties and studying the same subject as me, but we had never met before as she was a few semesters ahead. She had long brown curly hair and John Lennon glasses. I liked her right away. During our conversation she mentioned how difficult she found it to get to know people, despite the fact that there were thousands of other students around. 'You start a good conversation with someone and, then, when you ask them if they fancy going for a cup of coffee, they come up with all sorts of excuses, and that's it,' she said, just before the film started and we had to stop talking.

Those words were still ringing in my ears when the film ended. She asked me if I wanted to go for a cup of coffee. 'Yes, I'd love to,' I replied. We went to the student canteen, where we had some coffee from plastic cups. She told me that she was a lesbian. To her surprise, I didn't react in a shocked manner, but instead told her that I would probably consider myself to be bi. She asked me if I wanted to meet up again and, being very curious, and also still remembering her comment from before, I gave her my phone number. This was before mobile phones existed, and I was still living with my parents, which made me a little nervous.

A couple of days later, when I was at home studying, she called to ask me out to a local rock concert. I agreed to meet her that evening. I still remember sitting next to her in the concert, very distracted, my heart pounding and wondering how the evening might progress. My heartbeat didn't slow down after the concert when she suggested going to her place for a drink. As is very common in Germany, she shared an apartment with three other women. They each had their own room and shared a big kitchen. In Germany, most rooms in a shared apartment are quite spacious, and every room usually has a sitting area, writing desk and a sleeping area with a bed, shelves, etc.

Her room was no exception. She had just purchased a new bookshelf from IKEA the day before. She had assembled it that day and placed it right next to her bed.

We had been talking for a while, sitting on her couch, when Marion suddenly took her glasses off, leaned over and started kissing me. Oh my goodness, what a feeling! I'd never felt like that before. My heart stopped for a moment but, luckily, she didn't. Eventually, we ended up in her bed, next to her new bookshelf, which smelled intensely of new wood. It wasn't the most breathtaking sexual experience I have had in my life, but on the seventh day of the seventh month, 1977, when I spent my first night with a woman, I realised that it was possible to be with someone and be totally present, loving every moment. Needless to say, this evening changed a lot of things in my life, and also in my boyfriend's life – having to look for someone else to fulfil his fantasy being one of them.

Back to that day, more than 30 years later, when I found myself in the Irish Film Institute, as I was trying to tell myself that maybe I should just give up on ever seeing another woman, the smell of fresh wood reminded me of that special date, and I heard a voice inside me ask, 'Who are you trying to kid?'

Marlies McGuire

A Mother's Love Is a Blessing

Christmas 2008 and a Gay Old New Year 2009

He was the perfect guy. Truly perfect! What was wrong with me? I was spending Christmas with his family that year (we rotated Christmases between his family and mine). On Christmas Eve, he went out with his brother and father for a customary few pints before the man in the red suit arrived. I was staying in with his ma and five sisters. The boys left and, all of a sudden, the girls could no longer contain themselves. They let slip his surprise – Paris with a ring for my thirtieth! I was like a rabbit caught in the headlights. They all thought I was surprised with excitement, but it was the total opposite. I could hear Tom Hanks's famous words from *Apollo 13* swirling in my head: 'Houston, we have a problem.'

I was on total edge and, when the boys came back, I couldn't even look my boyfriend in the eye. My fake world was crumbling right under my toes. The guilt and shame I felt sent me straight into my head. For the next two days in his family home, I was unusually quiet. His mother and sisters put my withdrawn state down to being afraid I'd let slip their (his) surprise. He was worried about me, but I pretended that I was just missing my family at Christmas.

We left his family home on 27 December and went to visit my family. I was terrified. Everyone in my family loved him. They often referred to him as the perfect gentleman, and that

4

he was, but I was a lesbian. I knew what I had signed up for. I really thought I could do it, but all of a sudden the prospect of marrying a man, no matter how perfect he was, terrified me. What was I going to do? I spent the rest of the Christmas period in a pool of brandy, slipping between uncontrollable tears and absolute fear.

On 1 January, we made our way to our home together in Kildare. My head was full and my heart was aching. He knew something serious was up and, as soon as we got in the house, he asked me, 'What have I done wrong?'

It all happened so quickly. I can barely recall our conversation, but I blurted out, 'I'm gay.' The perfect gentleman was now the rabbit in the headlights.

He didn't know what to do; the values of a perfect gentleman don't allow for violence against women. But God bless the wall and doors because they sure did get it! For the first time in seven and a half years, I was afraid of him. He told me to leave immediately because he, too, was afraid of what he might do. His words said it all. 'If I'm found hanging from a bridge tomorrow, you remember whose fault it is!' So I left. I was 29 years old, and my lifetime lie had finally been exposed. I had no choice but to return home to my mam.

I arrived home with eyes red from sobbing. My mother gasped as I walked in and told her we'd broken up. I asked her if I could stay for a while, until I got sorted. I'll always remember my poor mother trying to console me. 'He'll take you back, it's normal to argue', etc., etc. But I didn't want him back, and this was far from a 'normal' argument.

I spent the next two weeks in bed, sobbing. What was I going to do? I was no longer able to hide my 'gayness'. It was oozing out of me with every tear and every thought. My mother was beside herself, not knowing what to do. She tried to call him, but he refused all our calls. Finally, I built up the courage to tell a couple of close family members my secret. They were all right about it, so long as I didn't go near them: 'Wink wink. Nudge nudge!' I explained to them that just because I was gay didn't mean incest was now a possibility, 'Wink wink. Nudge nudge!'

At the end of January, I avoided a family wedding because I couldn't handle the guilt and shame of what I had done to my boyfriend. The next day, a cousin called and asked me to go for a drive with her. I tried to resist but was given little option, so I agreed, and off we went on our drive. I'll never forget it. I was terrified, but I shouldn't have been. I'm from Westmeath, the lake county, and so we drove to one of the many lakes and took a stroll. As we were walking, my cousin turned to me and said, 'Lizzy, I don't know how to say this to you, but there was a rumour at the wedding that you're gay.' I nearly died on the spot. Those I had trusted had gossiped about me at the family wedding. My cousin continued, 'Lizzy, I don't care if we wake up tomorrow and you are purple with green spots. If you are gay, you are gay, not a monster and, to me, you'll always be my cousin.'

I burst out sobbing. Finally someone had accepted me for me, without my armour and, most important, without my lie. She told me that I had to tell my mother, I owed her at least that much. 'Tell her yourself,' she said. 'Don't let others carry your story with their own edits. And tell her as soon as possible, because the grapevine is buzzing with stories.' I decided I would tell my mother that day. My cousin offered to be there with me, but I felt I owed my mother the strength and courage to tell her on my own. I wanted her to feel she could react in whatever way she needed without having to tame her reaction because I had an ally in the room.

I went home and waited for my mother to return. I probably only waited for an hour, but it felt like a lifetime. She walked in the door, and I made her a cup of tea; tea fixes everything in our house. I asked her to sit down; I had something serious to tell her. She sat down, and I could feel her fear. I knew I couldn't beat around the bush with this one, so again I just blurted it out.

'Mammy, I'm gay!'

Her eyes filled with tears. 'Mammy, please don't cry,' I pleaded. 'I can't change this, but I will keep it hidden for you, just like I have for years.'

She looked up at me, took my hands to her heart and said, 'Lizzy, I'm not crying because you are gay. I'm crying because you finally know you are gay, and now I know you can be happy. I don't care that you are gay, but I do care about your happiness.' I fell into her arms, and she hugged me so hard I knew I would never have to hide again.

Thank you, Mammy, for allowing me to be me. I am so grateful to have such a wonderful mother.

P.S. The perfect gentleman never found it in his heart to forgive me, but I'm so glad he managed to heal enough to fall in love again. He's now happily married, and I am also grateful for that.

Lizzy

A Ribbon of Road (On the Road of Life)

'Name two forces of nature,' she said.

'Falling in love and a broken heart,' I answered.

'What about a volcano or an earthquake?'

'I have never experienced a volcano, and the earthquakes I have experienced have been powerful enough to rock my house, but not my world.' My friend Kathy and I sat talking under an August moon. Later, back at home, I began to recollect.

At the tender age of 23, I had fallen into what I reckoned was love, and, for two and a half years, my feet never touched the ground. When they finally returned to terra firma, it was with a bone-jarring slam. Lynette Murray held my affections, but announced that she did not love me. Plus, I did not have nearly enough money to accommodate her plans. As I had suspected, it was her, not me.

I was young, gay and living in Toronto. The city's aura of big-time excitement and the promise of unknown possibilities acted like a gravitational pull after high-school graduation. The LGBTQ scene was steadily progressing. Happily, it was becoming more accepted. Sadly, its edges appeared to be blurring into the mainstream. Being a card-carrying deviant was more 'meh' than menace now.

There had been many significant changes since the day I first arrived in the city, all fresh-faced and eager. The most noteworthy of these was when the provincial legislature passed an amendment to the Ontario Human Rights Code prohibiting discrimination against gay and lesbian people. However, it wasn't entirely a utopia; there were still causes to march for, including women's rights, AIDS research funding, Take Back the Night, and, of course, the annual Pride Parade, which had evolved into Pride Week. There were copious activities and groups that one could join, and there were the dance clubs, always the dance clubs. I imagined that I could be quite happy dancing my life away. Yet, despite it all, I could not have felt sorrier for myself or more undone.

For the first few weeks after the breakup, I would attend class and then flee back to my dorm to sob unabated into my pillow. There were moments when I fantasised about staying in my room forever and eventually fading away. Everyone would talk about my tragic demise from a broken heart and how awfully sad it was at such a young age. In reality, I knew that I was not serious about this course of action. First, there was my family to consider and, second, there was just so much that I wanted to do. One day, while walking down College Street, and beyond the cloud of angst hovering above my head, I spotted a poster in a shop window. It had a big, bright, colourful font and visually entertaining pictures promoting the fun and adventure of travel. A lightbulb went on in my head, and a revised life plan was born.

Thankful for a new purpose, I packed and repacked. What does one pack for a leap of faith? I ordered my first passport and purchased a travel book about Europe. Three months later I was working on a golf course in England. Nine months later I was on my way to mainland Europe; that was until I received a job offer from a golf course in Ireland. The position was to last four weeks, just long enough to replenish my travel funds. Eventually, that one month would morph into one year, but that was still a long way off.

After a night of travel from England through Wales, I eventually disembarked in Rosslare, my stomach queasy from the journey. Almost immediately, a voice inside my head said, 'Welcome home.' The source of that voice remains a mystery to me to this day. I found room and board at a home in County Kilkenny. The people were generous and friendly; the landscape

9

was green and rolling, and I had never worked so hard in my life!

Until I arrived in Ireland, I had never thought too extensively about the gay scene in other countries. Earlier that year, I had attended Euro Pride and investigated the nightlife in London and Paris, dancing in abundance in both cities. Those experiences left me optimistic that most European countries were pretty progressive in terms of LGBTQ acceptance. One morning, however, as I sat reading an Irish newspaper, I came across an opinion piece that waxed disparaging about the depravity of homosexuals. I felt sufficiently offended to write a letter to the editor. I had reached a point in my life where being indignant and seemingly 'the only gay in the village' was no longer enough for me; I felt the need to connect with a lesbian community. It was time to take a trip to Dublin or, as my co-workers referred to it, 'The Big Smoke'.

The following Saturday I arrived in a busy, sun-drenched Dublin. It had been raining relentlessly all week in Kilkenny, so this day felt almost decadent. I strolled down O'Connell Street, over the river Liffey and back again. I had my picture taken beside Molly Malone and at the entrance to Trinity College. Then I called the Gay Switchboard phone line. The fellow who answered said he wasn't sure but he thought there was a women's bar on Aungier Street, a place called JJ's. That evening, filled with anticipation, I made my way to the address that I had carefully written down. I was there, but JJ's was not. By the time I came on to the Dublin scene, it had closed and was now a jazz club. Lucky for me I liked jazz.

I boarded the bus for my return trip to Kilkenny, disappointed that I had not met even one lesbian. Soon afterward, I thought I should try meeting lesbian friends closer to home. I put an ad in the personals of the *Gay Community News* and received one reply. We arranged to meet at a café in Kilkenny city. Rita was 36, worked in the medical field and was not out to anyone. I told her about the letter I was drafting to the editor of the newspaper I'd read.

'I wouldn't send that to the newspaper if I were you,' she said.

'Why not?' I asked, incensed. 'Do you not find it outrageous that someone can write such malicious lies and get them printed?'

'Homosexuality is illegal in Ireland,' she replied.

'Illegal! It's the nineties!'

Rita just shrugged her shoulders and took a sip from her cup. That information was stunning. Rita and I spoke on the phone a couple of times after that day, but eventually we let our contact slip away. I still have the letter I drafted.

I later noticed in a gay newspaper that there was a women's discussion group in Dublin. God loves a trier! I phoned the number listed and was suddenly drawn into a clandestine scenario.

'Right, go to Books Upstairs,' instructed the woman on the phone. 'Stand in front of the bookstore; someone will approach you and direct you to a room in Trinity.'

I arrived in front of the bookstore at the allotted hour and stood in the dark, waiting. To my right was a woman in a black pea jacket and a Greek fisherman's cap. She was leaning against the wall of the building, and I sensed that she must be my contact. Then the fog rolled in. (I made that last bit up.) After a few minutes (and no fog), the woman walked over to me.

'Are you here for the discussion group?' she queried cautiously.

'Yes, I am,' I answered, in a half-whisper, perpetuating the cloak-and-dagger plot in my own mind.

'It's cancelled tonight,' she informed me.

'Noooooooooooo!' a voice howled silently in my head.

'If you don't mind waiting to see if anyone else shows up, we could go for coffee,' she offered.

Andrea turned out to be my good fortune. We talked about Ireland, Dublin, travelling, family – the conversation flowed easily. An hour into our coffee, she asked, 'Are you interested in going to a women's club?'

A club? A lesbian club, with real lesbians? 'Yes,' I answered; I most certainly was interested.

We set out and, after a short walk, entered a club located above a pub. Andrea introduced me to some of her friends, and I hit the dancefloor. Bliss! Later she asked if I wanted to go to another venue on the south side of Dublin. 'Lead the way,' I answered. We walked until we reached the canal, and then boarded a boat.

As I entered the cabin, the woman at the door proclaimed, 'You can stay until six, seven or eight in the morning, but I am kicking you out for nine o'clock Mass! Welcome to The Barge!'

I stood at the entrance looking around like I had never seen the inside of a boat before. Certainly never a boat anchored in a canal and filled with women. The best part about this, and subsequent visits, was that you could interact with everyone – students, academics, musicians, artists, women of every ilk.

Initially, I had misread the name painted on the side of the craft, and I asked Andrea, 'What is the name of this barge again? *Maid of the Alley*?'

'On some nights it is,' she replied, deadpan. As I recall, it was *Maid of the Allne*.

Sometime later, on another night out in Dublin, I narrowly averted disaster at a function in the Ormond Quay Hotel. While navigating through a room crowded with tables and people, I accidentally bumped into one of the tables. A big-boned woman standing beside the table glared at me ominously.

'Hey, Missus, do you want a punch in the face?' she asked.

Years before, while sitting in a doctor's office, I had read an article on parenting. The article said that parents should give their children the option of either one item or another, but not both. For example, a teddy bear or a doll, an apple or an orange. I tried that technique with my three-year-old niece, a notoriously fussy eater. I told her, 'You can have either the carrot or the pickle.' She chose the pickle, and everyone was happy. In my present predicament, I found myself thinking that the question 'Do you want a punch in the face?' left the possibility that there might be another option up for consideration, perchance no punch in the face. So I apologised to the woman and ended up in a 30-minute conversation about her cousin in America.

The gay scene was like that; there was always some adventure or misadventure to contemplate the next day.

This unexpected detour to Ireland left an indelible impression on me. Those initial four weeks and the following months were more life-altering than I could have planned. I was grateful for my job and the neighbours I had met, but I could scarcely wait for every second weekend to arrive, when I would travel to Dublin. It wasn't the drink, sometimes it was the dance, but always it was that sense of community and belonging that I felt while being around those women. In almost every way, the majority of them were strangers to me, but their journey was familiar. My home and native land was a long distance away, but Ireland was an endearing surrogate.

To my great surprise, and terror, love did come around again. This woman and this love were different from any that I had ever experienced. I did not recognise the power of the connection right away, but only because I was concentrating on keeping my feet firmly planted on the ground. This time I would not let them leave the ground. This time I used them to run all the way back to Canada! I spent several years wondering how my life would have been if I had only had the courage to defy one force and embrace the other. Recently, I had the opportunity to find out, but that is another story!

J.A. Valois

A Winter's Tale

I hear your key in the door as I peel and chop the last potato. The Thursday weariness of your voice when we spoke earlier on the phone whispered 'stew' to me. I slip my stockinged feet out of my domestic slippers and into heels as I walk to the door to greet you.

I take the satchel out of your hand and leave it on the floor with a thud. I unzip your winter coat and slip its dampness off your shoulders. I kiss you briefly, as I take your cold, red hand in mine and walk you upstairs. I check the bath I've already run in anticipation of your homecoming, and run a little more hot water into it. You stand in the doorway, weary, knowing the script we've written over the years, kicking off your shoes, knowing I want to do the rest. As I peel your damp clothes off your body, I become aroused. But not yet …

You sink completely into the scented bath and, when your head re-emerges, I lather it and massage it gently, expertly. I stand up as you re-submerge to rinse, and hand you a glass of warming Rioja – your favourite. I dim the lights and shut the door gently behind me.

It feels like a dance sometimes when we're together. Not a modern, improvised dance, but one we've spent time practising, negotiating, perfecting.

The first time I tried this particular routine, there was no silence, and I was met with a work-weakened resistance: 'You don't need to do this for me.' But, as time went on, and you learned to listen for the weary need in my voice and how to reciprocate, we both grew to learn the importance of our dance. To listen at random times to what would satisfy our needs, and our attentiveness leads to the grace and beauty of our dance.

I come back to you just as you begin to get restless. I don't need a clock to tell me when this is. You stand in the bath. I pull the plug and begin to towel you dry. I dry you well, between your toes, gently ruffling the towel through your hair, and lead you to our bed.

We kiss gently, deeply, for a long time, enjoying the often-underrated art of a good kiss. I move my mouth down your body, along your breasts, and ease your legs apart. My mouth finds your heat and moistness there and, as I inhale your scent, my tongue explores the familiar terrain of your body. You move gently at first and then push harder and faster against my face. My tongue moving deftly, my fingers pressing gently against you. I move up your body again, my hand replacing my tongue. Arching my back, I look at your face, your eyes are closed. Your pleasure pleasures me. I know you are close when your eyes shoot open. I love this face of yours – its intensity. As you moan, your eyes search my face; it is almost as if you can't believe what is about to happen. We move frantically. I push harder against you, into you and, then, when your body tells me, I gently ease out.

In the light of the street lamp, I turn over in your embrace and look at you. Your look can still melt me. I can feel the slippery satisfaction between my legs warming in your gaze. As we say our first words of the evening, I feel an explosion of pure, raw love splash inside of me.

'Dinner?' I ask, huskily.

'Stew?'

I nod.

'It'll hold,' you whisper, as you roll on top of me.

Susie Mortimer

An Uplifting Experience

It was a couple of months after our break-up. Smooth and easy break-ups are a rare happening. Mine was no different, except that, to me, ours was the only one in the world, and nobody could hurt as much as I did right now. Nine years later it still haunts me.

It was the day before Christmas Eve, and I had gone home. Was I in any way looking forward to Christmas? Absolutely not! I couldn't even muster the tiniest bit of enthusiasm. I had lost so much weight that none of my clothes would fit me. Normally, this would be a cause of great happiness and joy and lead to an eager dash to the shops to refresh my wardrobe and show off my new sexy body. But no. I was consumed and racked by a sadness and hopelessness that cut deep to the bone.

I barely existed, but I was trying hard to go through the motions and help with the Christmas preparations. Dropping Mum down to get her hair done, I wandered aimlessly around town and found myself looking at a lingerie shop. This was definitely a new departure for our little town and, as I found myself wandering into it, a very new departure for me. Crispy whites, stark reds, and the most beautiful satin blacks caught my eye. Suddenly, I caught sight of myself in a mirror and became extremely conscious that I looked a mess. In that instant, I became uncomfortably aware that not only were my clothes hanging off me but, as I twitched and wriggled, my bra was too.

I was stood still, more in a daze than in concentration, when all of a sudden a little voice pierced through my bubble.

'Can I help you there?'

'No thanks; I'm fine. Just looking.'

I wandered around, glancing at the really sexy nightwear. Maybe that's where I went wrong: I'd have never dared to wear anything so nice. Why didn't I put more effort into night-time? Over our ten years together, I didn't even buy her any special nightwear. I never tried to excite our bedtime.

The shop assistant was talking to me again, something about the new stock that had just arrived and what did I think of such and such. She handed me an open-lace – what I can only describe as fretwork – bra.

'Very nice,' I said, awkwardly, 'but I prefer just cotton.'

'Oh, we have that too! What's your size?'

'My what?' I looked blankly at her.

'Your size. What cup size do you take?'

No, I didn't say, 'Coffee or tea, thank you,' but I came damn close. 'Ahmm, I've lost weight,' I stuttered. 'I don't know.' That was my first mistake.

'Come on,' she chirruped. 'We can quickly sort that out.' A moment later, she was gently gripping my elbow and steering me into a changing room. A very small changing room. I stood zombie-like, blinking at my image in the mirror. The sales assistant disappeared for a moment, before reappearing with a tape around her neck.

'Now, pop off your jacket and jumper there, and we'll measure you up.'

I peeled off my jacket. The sweat was rising in me. Taking off my paint-splattered sweatshirt, I muttered, 'Sorry.' I muttered 'sorry' again as I saw her eyes catch my dirty T-shirt. She took a step closer and wrapped her arms around me. My breath stopped as she joined the ends of the measuring tape in front of me. I closed my eyes.

'Thirty-four C. Back in a sec.'

I looked at myself in the mirror. 'Christ, you're a mess,' I thought.

'Now, try these on. They're the latest. Pure cotton with the wire support. You'll need that to give you some lift,' she said kindly, in the flattest Dundalk accent. She started to remove the items from their packaging, and I lifted my T-shirt over my head, recalling in anguish my Mum saying, 'Don't you ever be caught with dirty underwear!' as I unveiled a practically threadbare, motley-grey, sagging bra. I was now beginning to blush with embarrassment. Wrenching both straps down as fast as possible, and struggling with the opening clips, my breathing became rapid and gasping. I dropped the offending item to the floor, using my foot to conceal it beneath my sweatshirt. I glanced at the assistant, glanced at my reflection, and noticed her polite, frozen smile as she handed me the new, freshly unpacked bra.

'Pop that on,' she said.

My eyes were now transfixed not on the new bra, but on the sagging, flat boobs facing me. I ever so quickly pulled my bra on, just as I had done every morning for the last 30-plus years, just as I probably would have continued to do for another 30 years – that is until a rather thinly raised teacher's voice rooted me to the spot.

'That is NOT how you put on a bra! Did your mother not teach you properly?'

Red, crimson, polka-dotted, call it what you will, my face was now burning with shame. Strawberry-faced, I looked down at my hands, which were entangled in the new bra. I tried to think straight, to figure out what the hell I was doing wrong. I've always done it this way. 'Mum, wait till I get you,' I thought. 'That's another form of neglect; you didn't teach me how to put a bra on!'

'You have to lift yourself into the cup,' the shop assistant continued. As she said this, her hands emerged from behind me.

'You must LIFT your breast into the cup like this.' Without any warning, she took hold of my breasts from behind and gently and tenderly raised them into their cups. I felt like I was dying. Slowly. But I very nearly did die when she suddenly blurted out, 'I know you! You taught me!'

She patted my breasts and grinned.

'There now. You even have a cleavage, Miss.' Twenty-four layers of crimson acrylic wouldn't give you the beetroot colour of my face.

'I do?' I spluttered. 'I mean, I did?'

'Do you not remember me? I came late every day to your class, just so you would notice me. Used to fancy you like hell. But, sure, I'm married now with kids. Here, you're looking a bit better than when you came in. Gimme that thing you were wearing; I'll be dumping that. And, if you don't mind me saying, I'll give you a deal on those bras. Think you need a few!'

I looked to my cleavage for inspiration. Raising my hands, I cupped my breasts and pushed upwards and inwards. A little valley transpired.

'I've got a cleavage,' I thought to myself, grinning shyly. The sales assistant caught my eye in the mirror as she reappeared with the other bras.

'Olive, that's my name, Miss. Bet you'll remember me now!'

I so do remember you, Olive. I quite fancied you too!

Caroline Bond

Art

I went to the Arteskola for the first time when I was about ten or twelve. Calling it an art school was more aspirational than accurate. The Academy was an old garage with uneven concrete floors, swinging, naked lightbulbs, and buckets placed strategically in anticipation of the rain. The attendance fee was something like €8 per year, possibly even €5. The ancient (as they seemed to my young self) men who ran the school appeared to be in the same state of precariousness as the building itself. It wasn't until many years later that I came to see my three teachers at the school as the beautiful, epic heroes they undoubtedly were.

In my home town, in the Basque Country, art and culture were alien concepts. There was no cinema in my town, and there was no public library. After Francisco Franco's death in 1975, democracy returned, and Basque nationalists ran local government. One thing did not change, however: contempt for the provision of public art and culture. Funny that the same attitude is quite widespread in my second home, Ireland, at the present time, 2012.

The invisibility of art during my childhood and adolescent years was particularly ironic because in every single household in my town, in the most prominent room, on the wall with the best lighting, and bestowed with the most expensive and exquisitely finished made-to-order frame, hung the same cubist painting: Pablo Picasso's *Guernica*. Sounds surreal? It was! But I only realised that later, when I studied art history. When I was growing up, it felt perfectly natural to me to have this black-and-white arrangement of horrifying entangled shapes staring at me from every living room, anteroom, hall and meeting room in my home town. It was as natural as the very air, as natural as the arched walkways in the town centre, the ridged grey cobbles on the streets, or the cast-iron god 'Mercury', which stood on a fountain by the main crossroads. As I also discovered during my student years, this was, in fact, a sculpture of Bacchus, and an interesting example of self-denial in a town of dedicated drinkers.

Why on earth was the painting everywhere, you may well ask. And it is a perfectly valid question. But let me linger briefly here, before the mystery is solved, so I can encourage you to reflect on how some things feel natural simply because we grow up with them. How even the most bizarre occurrences, the most shocking images, can feel as commonplace, non-descript and excitement-free as a slice of slightly stale bread left on the kitchen table. Conversely, something as appalling and distressing as the lack of art and culture provision in a community that considers itself to be civilised can feel as normal as the lack of a sixth finger on one's hand, or the lack of a third eye on one's face. And what is true of art is true of other things. Many of us grew up never hearing the word 'lesbian', and were consequently unable to imagine it, not knowing that the normalcy of our common experiences ceased the second we stepped over a certain radius. Many of us grew up not suspecting that some boring and familiar things were in fact warnings, a shorthand for forgotten and coming catastrophes, for the casual cruelties humans specialise in. Public and private cruelties.

Very well, then. Why was Picasso's *Guernica* staring back at me everywhere in my town? Simply because my home town is called Gernika. You may have guessed that this is the Basque spelling of 'Guernica'. And you may know that this is the name of a town bombed by the Nazis in April 1937, during the Spanish Civil War, an experiment in decimating from the air a civilian population of no military or strategic value. Picasso had been commissioned to make a painting to represent Spain (democratic Spain, under attack from fascist forces) at the

International Exhibition in Paris, and he chose to show to the world what had happened in Gernika. Franco's side officially declared that we Basques had burned down the town ourselves. After 1975 in Gernika, it seemed to me that the broken cubist bodies and buildings in the painting were clearly legible to anyone, whether they had an interest in art or not.

Of course, it didn't automatically follow that the kind of analysis, communication, learning and entertainment that art and books provide should have thrived in a town that had embraced Picasso. Yet, perhaps you will agree that the scene of my art-phobic town covered with cubist posters is rather strange. The painting has always been associated with this historical tragedy, but it can also be seen as a denunciation of any random targeting of a community. A denunciation of homophobia, too, perhaps. Let my story then be a contribution to the 75th anniversary of the bombing this year.

At the Arteskola, a single educational strategy was implemented: copying. In pencil, on our precious sketchbooks, we copied from a series of photocopied images depicting landscapes, objects, flowers, buildings, animals, human faces, etc., and we tried our hands at progressively more complex arrangements of lines, carefully supervised by our tutors. We might spend some weeks on a set of poppy flowers, for example, some months on a sleeping dog. After a few years of this – perhaps four – the big day would come, unannounced and unexpected. Suddenly, we would be formally invited to the space at the back of this open-plan garage, leaving the rows upon rows of desks we had previously occupied behind us for good. The space at the back, which had always seemed as remote and blurry as Mount Olympus, held a collection of sculptures, plaster copies of classic artworks. There was the boy pulling a thorn out of his foot, the discus thrower, and a rather unattractive (I thought) Apollo. We must have had a Venus de Milo too, though (oh dear) I have forgotten her.

On that side of the garage, in a state of great trepidation, we were each allocated a boarded easel and handed in turn a large piece of brown paper, a rag and a stick of charcoal. Then the copying resumed. For a few more years we copied, from our immutable three-dimensional models, perhaps an arm, the folds in some drapery, a bit of hair behind an ear, maybe a torso and, occasionally, a full body set at an unusual angle. What could have been a training in love, in the jolt of finding beauty in all places, was instead the learning of un-yearning, a programming in proportioning, the cloning of coldness. We got better and better at establishing distances and equivalences, things that could be translated – translated from the mutilated outside world of eggshell eyes, into our very own private space of unrolled, torn brown paper. And by God did we excel at it!

This was not quite the end of the training in the Arteskola. Something even more unimaginable beckoned from another corner at the back of the garage: oil painting. Older people (perhaps in their twenties and thirties) populated this area, an area that again had seemed to me to be as far away and as unconquerable as Pluto when I was stuck copying sculptures. And, now, here I was. A teacher showed me some books with reproductions of classical paintings for me to choose from. To copy, of course. I threw myself into it with the commitment and sense of responsibility of one who knows herself to be privileged. It was as if some great mercy had been shown to me, as if I had been presented with a winged horse or eternal life, as if my name had been announced at the entrance to a ball with all of history's great painters in attendance. What else could matter in the world, other than this, other than art? I remember my utter grief and misery when the only art shop in town ran out of indigo paint. But I was stuck; I needed a tube of blue paint at all costs. So, I had to buy the heartbreakingly hideous ultramarine instead. I lived in a house of the mind built of these ecstasies and disappointments.

And, in the midst of all this excitement, came the Big Bang, the big, bold beginning of my being. It occurred one evening in autumn, as I was walking home through the square after my art class, in the gently darkening air. I happened to notice a change in the light, so I looked up. And there she was. How had I not seen her before? A big, fat, shiny moon, far away above me, peeking through the uncertain clouds. Was she looking at me too? It didn't even matter. I was enthralled. She was so beautiful. So present. It felt as though there were just the two of us in the universe. This thing above me, this thing shaped like the moon, surrounded by clouds, was real. It was there, and I was looking at it.

Suddenly, I knew what I had to do. I fumbled in my bag and found a scrap of paper and a pencil. Then, uncertainly, eagerly, I drew the moon. Let me tell you, it was not a pretty drawing. You would scarcely have guessed what it was meant to be. It seemed more like a weird blotch, with washed-out, elongated stains and an odd, round-shaped empty space in the middle. But it was real. And I had drawn it myself. It was not a copy of a copy, a thousand times repeated for a thousand years. It was something I had chosen to draw, something with more life in it than all the flowers, all the dogs, all the feet and all the faces I had drawn and painted throughout my years in the art school.

And this moment was the beginning of me as a person. I have sometimes wondered where my lesbianism came from, and I think it came from this. From giving myself permission not to copy. From looking at the world for what it is. That was the first step; only then was I ready to invent. Was it by chance that I picked the moon as my badge? After all, it is the symbol of Diana, or Artemis, the lesbian goddess.

Some years later, I was speaking with a friend. 'I have been wanting to tell you something,' I said. 'I think I have fallen in love with a woman.'

'I see,' she said. 'I have been wanting to tell you something, too. I have been in a relationship with a woman for the past two years.'

What are the chances? Could it be true? Could women have relationships with women? Could women have sex with women? Could they love each other? Be together? This could only happen outside the world of photocopies and plaster casts and colour reproductions. This could only happen in the world of colour.

Many years later, as I queued outside a toilet in a bar, I noticed a woman I was mad about in the queue before me. We started discussing periods. I remember her militant rant against the inadequate provision for sanitary-towel disposal and my passionate defence of tampons. Then, a few moments later, as I stood by the toilet seat, about to discard my used tampon, I noticed a freshly discarded sanitary towel in the waste basket. Who could have resisted it? Merging the warm tones on a round palette, dropping the red on the red – it was art that made me do it. What I did was art.

Another time, I remember having a drink with some friends, including an ex whom I had been trying very hard to un-fancy. I was succeeding spectacularly, totally absorbed in a conversation about current affairs with someone else, until, out of the corner of my eye, I noticed her long glass and what she was doing to it. Her index finger went up and down, up and down the length of the glass, up and down, before she stopped and rested it on the rim, which she then circled with her thumb, while her little finger tapped on the side. Then, again, her index finger went up and down, up and down … how could I not be hypnotised by the criss-crossing of those lines? The verticals, the perpendiculars, the curves, the repetition? It was just like drawing with a charcoal stick: the fingers carefully spreading the dust to make shades, the white chalk mixing with the charcoal, the rubbing and soft blowing of the dust and the gentle flicker of a cloth on the paper. Sip after sip, her glass of water was getting empty, and simultaneously, in exact proportion, mine was getting full. It was a case of artistic appreciation and aesthetic empathy.

On another occasion, I remember hugging my girlfriend in the street. We stood for a long time, embracing in a tender, slow-motion, south-wind, Sunday-afternoon sort of way. I remember asking if this was what being married felt like and not wanting to ever release from our embrace. We held hands just so we could walk away from the hug. That moment was truly special. It was not hollow, not plaster, not photocopied, not reproduced, and not calculated. Unfortunately, it was also not to be repeated.

Here, in Lesbianland, people are like moons, and they draw cushion clouds to rest their heads. Here, azure women pace under trees, waiting for a vermillion hour. Here, chalks and charcoals, like conducting batons, bring themselves and each other into a frenzied silence. Here, in Lesbianland, true Art rules.

Written on the 75th anniversary of the bombing of Gernika, Basque Country.

Aintzane Legarreta Mentxaka

Dreams Do Come True

Have you ever tried to drift off to sleep by making a very deliberate effort to think pleasant thoughts about what you would like to happen in your life? Maybe you like to think about meeting the love of your life? Winning the lottery? Becoming a famous movie star? Starting a family? OK, I'll stop there before I get too carried away. Whatever about our adult fantasies and dreams, can you recall any of your childhood dreams?

Just picture a five- or six-year-old child not able to sleep at night for some reason. Maybe the reason is that the child is fully immersed in a religion that has instilled fears in them about going to hell – who knows? It's almost impossible to recall our childhood experiences with any understanding of the emotions or thoughts that were going on in our little heads at the time.

One way of 'saving' myself from going to hell was to sleep with my arms folded across my heart, shoulder to shoulder. Someone must have told me that folding your arms in this way was like wrapping yourself in the protection of your angels. The comfort provided by my angels allowed me drift off into my own little world, where I could strip off my mask and just be me. 'I will wake up in the morning, and I will be a girl,' I thought. 'My curly hair will be shoulder-length and held back from my face with a pretty hairband. I'll skip off to school in my pinafore and white knee socks, looking forward to a new day of learning, fun and friendship.'

For some time – God only knows how long – this wasn't really a wish or dream; I was convinced that it was going to happen. It was just a matter of time until the 'problem' was resolved, and the confusion about how I dressed and how my hair was cut would be sorted out once and for all. Was I the only six-year-old who understood that the difference between boys and girls was as simple as that fact that boys have short hair and girls have long hair? I have no recollection of ever telling anyone about my dilemma and, certainly, I have no memory of anyone telling me that my expectation to live my life as a girl was wrong. But, in some way, I knew I had to hide my true self and continue with the pretence that I was a boy, at least until everyone else realised the mistake.

In May 1964, at the age of six and a half, I made my First Holy Communion. Do you remember how important the half was when you were that age? Heck, I have just given away my age to anyone who can do the maths! I couldn't understand why I wasn't on the right-hand side of the church in a beautiful white dress. You can immediately see how devoted I was to my religious instruction: 'The Holy Eucharist be dammed! Why the hell am I not my angelic self in a silk, knee-length dress, veil and white patent shoes?' I can recall with amazing clarity my sadness at being excluded from a little girl's experience of being the focus of attention on that special day. Yes, that's me, always the attention-seeker! My Communion was the first time I realised I was trapped in a boy's world. But growing out my hair and wearing pretty dresses wasn't about to happen any time soon.

Trying to drift off to sleep at night, my expectations soon become pleas for some magical or miraculous intervention by my angels. I created endless innocent scenarios of me wishing that boys could also wear pretty dresses and ribbons in their long hair. This preoccupation with presenting and dressing as a girl was always my entrance ticket to the girls' world. It would give me permission to play with the girls and allow me to escape the rough and tumble of the boys' world, where I was constantly afraid. Being called a sissy was the worst thing in the world for a boy. Showing fear – fear of falling off a wall, fear of ghost stories, fear of being caught robbing the orchard – was the one sure way of attracting a bully and ending up being labelled a sissy.

Fast-forward a number of years, when my childhood innocence was replaced by the realities of puberty. The distinction between boys and girls was suddenly more pronounced, and I became more and more excluded from the life I longed for. At the same time, I was on the periphery of the boys' world that I was expected to inhabit. The joy of my younger self's innocent fantasies was soon replaced by guilt and self-loathing. Suppression of my true self became the order of the day and was my one and only survival strategy. I buried my core identity to a level that allowed me to believe that I was normal, that I was male.

I was very good at this pretence and constantly set tasks and objectives that would prove (to myself) that I was male. I played rugby, reasonably well, well enough to get on the junior and senior cup teams. But reality was always bubbling away just below the surface of my pretence. The rugby changing room was a hotbed of male testosterone, where I could just about hide the truth from my teammates, but not from myself. Looking at the macho performances of the other lads – their boasts about their many conquests and the size of their penises, their ability to drink, and their constant sexual references to girls – always managed to prick through my protective shield and remind me of my true identity. I still had trouble sleeping at night and would often cry myself to sleep with my arms folded across my chest in the angelic position of my childhood. During the day, I snatched moments of peace and tranquillity from waking dreams of a magic potion that would complete my male-to-female transition.

The start of college happened to coincide with my first long-term relationship, the first relationship I had had of any duration. Hey, a girl at last showed an interest in me! Her older brother had told me that she fancied me. If it hadn't been for his intervention, we would never have gotten together. I thought this was the answer to all my problems. How could I be anything other than normal if a girl fancied me? Wow! How could an eighteen-year-old be so naive? Ellen was a tomboy. She was intelligent, kind and big-hearted. And she may have been a lesbian desperately trying to be straight.

My interest in all things girlie got its first chance for expression when I persuaded Ellen to experiment with her wardrobe and try a more feminine style of dressing. The truth is that I was using Ellen to live out my own second-hand feminine experience. Of course I was male; I wouldn't fancy Ellen if I was female. Lesbians didn't exist in the mid-1970s. Retrospection is cruel – such lack of understanding and efforts at self-delusion seem so foolish now but, at the time, it seemed pretty plausible.

Ellen dumped me after two years, and we lost contact. I never did find out if she was a lesbian. I think she married the guy she dumped me for, but experience has taught me that that doesn't prove anything.

Devastated by the rejection, and still crippled by guilt about my gender issues, I once again upped the suppression level. 'I might be a little kinky, I might find dressing as a woman a turn-on, but I am not a woman. I repeat, I am not a woman! I am normal. I am not a weird transsexual.' No matter how hard I tried to resist, I was constantly drawn back to my innocent childhood beliefs that I was female. There is nothing sordid or seedy about the thoughts and aspirations of a child. Later on in life, these childhood recollections helped save my sanity when I put myself through aversion therapy in an effort to 'cure' my 'illness'. 'Suppress, suppress, get on with your life! I fancy girls; I'm a man.' I know this story reads as though I have a slight blind spot when it comes to lesbians and, OK, I admit I'm a little on the slow side; I have led a sheltered life. Is that a good enough way of explaining away my ignorance?

Dream, dream, dream, and one day your dreams will come true. That is what I believed. I was 23 years old at this stage, and my angels were still working on my miracle transition. You didn't think I was going to do anything practical, did you? Like talking to a doctor or a psychologist? No. I set about finding a girlfriend who would, once and for all, give me all the proof I needed that I was, in fact, male. I met, fell in love with, and married Niamh by the age of 25. We spent the next 25 years doing our best to act out the roles we had assumed. Niamh was trapped in a marriage with a pretend man who had conned her. I try to mitigate my guilt about deceiving Niamh by rejoicing in the two wonderful daughters we have brought into this world.

All this time, my coping strategy – in between bouts of depression – was to spend blissful moments of escapism visualising myself living as Paula. I had no idea how it was going to happen, and I still hadn't managed to talk to anyone other than Niamh about my deeply held belief that I was female. Well, if it wasn't for a stroke at the age of 50, I can't imagine ever taking the first steps on my transition journey.

My body had finally decided enough was enough. With no history of heart problems or high blood pressure, the stroke was a complete bolt from the blue. A switch went off in my head and temporarily shut down my analytical brain. This momentous event allowed my heart to take over and bring my gender concerns out into the light. It has been a slow but fulfilling journey where, for the very first time in my life, I have started to like who I am. At all stages of this transition, I have encountered amazing people who have guided me and helped me on my way. It has only taken me 50-odd years to realise that there isn't an answer to every question. Wiser people than me have changed the way I see life and have opened my eyes to endless possibilities. These people know who they are, and many of them are members of Running Amach. I will be eternally grateful to all who have shown me kindness, provided words of encouragement, accepted me as a friend and, of course, blessed me with loads of hugs. My angels finally discovered the potion that would make my dreams come true.

My life has changed so much since this was written in April 2012.

Paula

Finding My Sparkle

I have had a lot of questions over my adult life, some of which I still cannot answer. I have, however, taken a journey that has made me appreciate the extreme diversity of our society and the difficulties we are faced with in our efforts to be accepted for who we are. People often ask me when I came out. Simple as the question is, I struggle to answer it. What does the term 'coming out' actually mean? Does it require me to declare to the world that I'm gay, or am I qualified as 'out' when I've shared my sexual preference with select people? In fact, why do we have to fall into a category at all? Gay, straight or bisexual, can't we just be people who like to have physical and emotional relationships with other people? Which leads on to my most frustrating question: if I am gay, how do I explain my being attracted to boys in the past? We don't suddenly become gay; we're born that way, right? Has part of my brain now realised that I like women and, therefore, switched itself off to men? Did I only think I liked these guys, or did I somehow change over the years? I'm 35 years old, and these questions still puzzle me.

It's hard to know where it all began. The above questioning certainly began well into my adult life, at the age of 23, when I started to realise my attraction for women, or one particular woman at that time. That said, I now recognise that my first feelings for women existed as far back as primary school. I have a vague recollection of enjoying being around a sub-teacher, for no reason other than that she was nice and made me giggle a lot. Moving into secondary school, I had a definite crush on my PE teacher. My naive little mind did not have the sense to acknowledge any of these as lesbian tendencies. It was only during my final year of university that things started to take a twist.

Up until that point, I had never been in a relationship. The closest I got was a two-week 'thing' with a guy who my friends convinced me was a good match for me. They even had me brainwashed into thinking that I possibly did like him deep down, so I figured I should at least give it a go. Although, I was pretty sure this advice was a load of bollocks, I didn't understand quite how far-fetched it was until I met a girl and felt that magical spark for the first time.

I was recruiting girls for a new university GAA football team, and that's how Jen came into my life. We were introduced by a mutual friend, and – although I didn't admit to it at the time – I was instantly attracted to her. I couldn't explain what was going on; suddenly, I felt this fire inside of me that I had never felt before. But I was 23 years old. Surely, if I was gay, I would have known about it before now? Or does this explain why I've always felt that things were not quite right? Is this what I had been missing all along?

Jen and I became close friends very quickly, though it took her some time to build up the courage to tell me that she 'kicked with the other foot', to quote her exact words. I had guessed it fairly early on, but I was too afraid to raise the subject, given my own feelings. When she did eventually tell me, I made a shambles of things. She revealed that she was attracted to me, and I went into denial. I told her I was not attracted to women, but that I would like to be her friend. I was ashamed of my reaction, particularly after having seen how difficult it was for Jen to open up like that, but I had to protect myself; I couldn't let myself become vulnerable and move into the unknown. I was afraid I would lose all control of who I was. Basically, I chickened out. I wondered if this was simply a phase I was going through. I mean, what if it turned out that I wasn't really gay after all, by which point I would have led her up the garden path? That was my defence for not having been open and honest.

Jen then started to become more comfortable with her sexuality, and soon started seeing a friend of mine, a 'straight' girl to whom I'd introduced Jen a few months earlier. I suddenly found myself feeling jealous, and it was then that I knew this was more than just a phase. I really liked this girl! I tried to hide it, but Jen picked up on the vibes. She eventually ended their relationship, but didn't explain why, leaving my friend wondering what she had done wrong. I found myself in an awkward situation, because my friend knew nothing about my feelings for Jen, and I had to be there for her when Jen dumped her. Guilt started piling up big-time; my head was all over the place.

Jen and I eventually got together in the last few weeks of term. It was inevitable, really; we were hanging out almost every day and becoming increasingly sentimental about leaving university and going our separate ways. The first night we kissed was probably the highlight of my five years at college. For the first time in my life, it felt so right. Despite the perfection of the first kiss, my freaking-out period started pretty much the next day.

I pondered the situation for a few days and, eventually, I just had to talk to someone. I told a few of my closest friends. This was the first I had spoken of even having had feelings for Jen. I felt such relief to be able to let it out. My friends were very supportive and gave me the time I needed to figure things out. Jen and I had a secret relationship for four months during the summer of 2000, until I left the city and moved back home. We kept in touch for a while, but I eventually received a phone call to say that she had met someone else. I felt like my world had ended.

It took me a long time to get over Jen. By this point, I had moved to Dublin because I couldn't handle living at home with my God-fearing parents who, in my opinion, could not cope with the knowledge of having a gay daughter. I was holding down two jobs to help pay back student debts, I had no social life, and I lived with my sister, who knew nothing of what was going on. I tried, on a number of occasions, to tell her, but I always chickened out. I was really struggling, but she had no idea. The only three people in the world who I could talk to were no longer around me physically. One friend was back in the city where I studied, one was back home, and the other was in Australia.

My struggle continued for about three years, during which time I would occasionally kiss a guy just so I wasn't causing people to talk. I made some minute steps towards progress, but the main obstacle holding me back was my fear. I eventually told all my closest friends, but I still struggled to act on any advice given to me. I became comfortable in knowing that I was gay, but I was in absolute trepidation of my mother and father finding out. I would not venture near any gay venue or event for fear of being seen by someone from back home. Eventually, I made the decision to never tell my parents, so I stopped worrying about how that conversation would pan out. I also relaxed more about feeling any obligation to tell people at all. I wasn't with anyone, so what news was there to tell, really? This helped me to stop dwelling on the subject. Over time, I became more tolerant about letting people know my secret, but I lived off the hope that those who knew would have the common sense not to leak such gossip to my elderly parents. Progress, yes. Out – certainly not!

My only experience of the gay scene was from weekend breaks or holidays with friends. Before long, each trip away with friends became a huge mission to check out the gay scene, all for my benefit. In most cases, I arrived home disappointed, either because we couldn't find the venues or because the bars were dark and seedy and very male-dominated. Given my very limited exposure to anything gay, my encounters with women were obviously very sparse. I did, on occasion, take the plunge and go to The Front Lounge (the local gay bar) with friends, but it was impossible to meet people in that kind of environment. Plus, it didn't help that my dear friends were on a mission to pull me a woman. I never met a woman that way, nor did I see any girls that I was particularly attracted to. I did start to develop feelings for a friend of a friend who was straight, though, or so she would like to believe. We had a 'thing' one night after I opened up to her, but it all backfired after she revealed that she was merely wanting to satisfy her curiosity about what it was like to be with a woman.

I eventually plucked up the courage to come out to my sister. I have to say, this was my most difficult coming-out experience to date. She was shocked, but took it very calmly and assured me that she wouldn't treat me any differently. Days and weeks passed, and she never raised the subject. Eventually, I did, and she made it clear that she never wanted to discuss it. She was clearly very uncomfortable with it. When my friends would come with me to a gay bar, my sister would refuse to go. She wasn't homophobic as such; in fact, she has a male gay friend and accompanies him to gay bars; it was just an issue that I was her sister. It's funny, she is just one and a half years older than me, but we have never talked about certain intimate things.

As the years went on, I lost my dad after a long illness, and I began to find myself avoiding going home so often to my mother's house. While Dad was ill, my sister and I had spent alternating weekends at home to give Mum a rest. But now that I did not need to be around as much, I was able to escape most of the questions from neighbours, such as, 'Any men on the go?' or, 'Any word on you getting married yet?' I now visit home once every six to eight weeks, but I do feel that I have become a little bit of a stranger within the family. I guess I can't have it all ways, so it's a price I have to pay, at least until I decide to come out to everyone.

By the time I turned 30, I started to look at meeting people online. I was very wary of online dating, so I set up my profile to indicate that I was looking to meet like-minded people in order to build up a circle of friends on the gay scene. I found it very difficult to gauge who was genuine from the site, and so I tended to have extended email conversations with people before suggesting any face-to-face meetings. I only ever agreed to meet two people. I was stood up on my first planned meeting and, as a result, I developed a complex that she had seen me and decided to do a runner.

With my confidence knocked, I left the site and went into hiding for another year. I eventually gave the online search another shot, and my first new buddy was called Sara. She subsequently became my girlfriend. Sara, like me, was struggling with coming out. She was in a worse position, though; she had never kissed a woman, and she had not opened up to anyone about how she was feeling. She was in the same place that I had been seven years earlier, and I was the only person in the world she could talk to. I told my sister about Sara, but she made it clear that she did not want to meet her or hear anything about our relationship. I lived with my sister at the time, so you can imagine how fun it was trying to dodge her in the middle of the night if Sara stayed over.

Sara and I had gotten together pretty quickly, but hindsight reveals that we were not right for each other. We got together for the wrong reasons. Perhaps we needed each other at the time, but as I grew to learn more about myself, I came to the realisation that I wanted her as a friend and not a lover. Although I knew Sara and I had done the right thing by ending things, I became very lonely after our break-up, and fell back into my world of depression. I missed her and found myself wanting to get back with her. In fact, we did get back a few months later for a short spell, after which Sara ended it. I soon understood that my issue was that I didn't want to go back to being alone again. After almost two years of companionship, I had forgotten what being alone felt like.

My sister didn't know about our break-up, so I wasn't able to go to her for support. It was at this point that I moved into my own apartment. Much as I love my sister, I knew that I had too many of my own problems to be able to deal with her issues as well. If I was to ever meet someone and be myself, I had to be in a comfortable environment.

My second move in the right direction was my decision to go for counselling. Friends made me aware of my openness to talk about my feelings and suggested that all I needed was someone to prompt me with the right questions. Counselling helped me focus on what was really bothering me. In the previous ten years of learning to understand and become comfortable with my sexuality, I suddenly discovered that I did not really know myself and was not at all comfortable about being gay. I had never frequented gay venues or spent time in the company of gay people. I struggled with my identity as a Catholic and didn't know what to believe any more. I started to question my career and my abilities. I had lost all confidence in myself. I read online about the Outhouse organisation, and went along to the Thursday women's night. I brought Sara along, since she also needed to get out and meet other people. Before long, we both started to make some mutual friends, but it soon became apparent that Sara and I needed space from each other.

It was then that I joined Running Amach, and this became the turning point of my coming-out journey. I made an immediate friend through Running Amach and, thanks to her, I attended my first Pride Parade in 2010. What an amazingly memorable day! For the first time, I was out with like-minded people and feeling totally comfortable with being 100 per cent myself. It wasn't long before I began to immerse myself in everything gay. I went to meetups that I would not typically attend and, through this, learned so many things about myself that I would not have experienced had I not ventured into the unknown. I became a busy bee, attending multiple events. I was determined to make up for the previous nine years of sheltered existence in Dublin.

Now, almost two years on, I am a happier person. My sister is beginning to become more at ease with my sexuality, and she has met some of my gay friends. I have been considering coming out to more people in my family, a thought that I would not have entertained two years ago. I'm even beginning to warm to the idea of possibly telling my mother at some point, though I'm just taking things one sure step at a time.

This is not the end of my story, not by a long shot. I have, however, made progress, and I am continuing to take forward steps, so life is going in the right direction. After a wasteful decade of needless fear and dread, I feel liberated, and I have begun to find my sparkle. I am learning new things about myself every day, and I am more passionate about the future.

As for the multiple questions still going around in my head, maybe I will never be able to answer them, but that's OK. No matter what, I am extremely proud to be a Running Amacher!

Tess

First Love Attacks the Heart

My journey began in my second year at grammar school. I was thirteen. It turned out to be a terrible year, but a year that offered many challenges and obstacles that I eventually overcame. I was your average youth, not a delinquent, yet not one to follow the conventional path. I had never questioned my sexuality; it all seemed too constricted at that stage. I never allowed myself to think outside the box. But then I met her – the girl who would change me, my perspective and my outlook on love. Ultimately, she would be the first girl to break my heart into a thousand pieces.

Claire had the most piercing blue eyes, her golden-blonde hair was exquisite, and her mind – even at her age – was incredible. We had been friends for a long time, but I never thought we would be anything more. It all began with a bet that my friend Helen and I had made to kiss a girl. 'Yuck' was the first thought that came to my mind; yet, later, the prospect became more enticing.

At the time, my aunt was very sickly and ill; my mother was away looking after her. I was staying at Claire's house and, as usual, we were joking around, doing our homework and chatting about the things teenagers chat about. She was beautiful, but the truth is I was oblivious to just how beautiful she actually was. We finished up our work, and it was time for bed. As usual, when the lights went out, the real conversation began.

Claire loved to talk, although that night she seemed a little silent, a little distracted. Finally, she turned to me and asked if

I was OK. My mum had phoned earlier with news of my aunt. It wasn't going well for her, and I had been upset by the news. I told Claire I was fine. She just laughed the awkwardness off, and then she sprung it on me. She asked about the bet that I had made with Helen. I was stunned; I didn't even know how she'd heard about it. She said she was a more-than-willing participant, but I just couldn't take her seriously. It all seemed a bit surreal. How had we reached this point? She looked at me and laughed, telling me that I was too scared to actually go through with it. The challenge was there, but so was my inner conflict.

Eventually, after many failed attempts, after watching the minutes and hours tick away on the clock radio, I summoned up the courage, leaned over, closed my eyes and kissed her. The moment our lips met, it felt like the world had stopped. I was trembling – whether out of fear or excitement, I can't say. The kiss was passionate, yet gentle and thought-provoking. It felt like we had been entwined for an eternity before we emerged from our embrace.

I opened my eyes briefly and they met hers. Still overwhelmed, I quickly turned around and pretended to sleep. The kiss had been electrifying but, eventually, after convincing myself it had just been an illusion, I drifted off to sleep. I awoke the next morning startled to discover that Claire was, in fact, there. Our kiss was suddenly removed from the surreal world and brought straight into reality.

I tried to avoid her and the topic of our kiss for a long time, but I eventually stopped dancing around the issue and we kissed again. This time, we continued to kiss. The rush, the compassion, the caresses, they seemed to linger on our skin. Her way of telling me it was getting serious was making me watch an advertisement for a video game with the slogan 'It's beyond a game'. She was innovative, creative and sensational. Yet I continued to battle my inner conflict. I was so indecisive. Not about the way I felt about her, but about the way society and my family would feel about me if the truth was ever brought to light. But the truth was that my heart swelled with love for her. She had become the centre of my teenage world. My thoughts were stuck on her, and she showered me with affection that seemed endless.

To every new beginning, however, there seems to be a big, dramatic end. Such is the way of all teenage sagas. Our relationship ended on less than good terms. She had given me so much – magical memories, mystical moments and, at one stage, even her heart. Though that young love was so long ago, your first young love truly captures your heart. Mine held me prisoner for more than three years. That is until I met the next girl ...

Chris McMurray

From Russia with Love

The text came in at about 2:30 p.m., just as I was browsing around Eason's bookshop on O'Connell Street. It read: 'Hi hope you are good today and not work too hard, I am off, enjoy your day.' As I read it, I could hear the broken English accent and her rolled Rs. It was from Maria, a beautiful Russian woman I had met the previous Sunday when I brought her to the lesbian swimming group Swimmin Wimmin.

Maria was about 5'8", with flaming orange hair that fell just below her shoulders. She had a lovely face, with high, well-defined cheekbones, chocolate-brown eyes that had a slightly oriental characteristic, sallow skin, and a smile that could light up a room. She was, in a word, gorgeous, with the body of an Olympian – a fact I discovered that Sunday when she changed into her very minute bikini with thong. She was very embarrassed by this when she realised that the rest of us were wearing our very sensible, all-in-one Speedos. I was amused to see the bikini, but I have to say I did scan her over once or twice with an eye of definite appreciation, and I wasn't the only one. There were a few other sideways glances before she wrapped her towel around her waist and headed to the pool, where she slipped the towel off and made her way graciously down the steps into the water like some Greek goddess.

So, there I was in Eason's, getting a text from this stunner, and I could hardly contain my excitement. I sent back a text: 'Hi, I am having a good day. I'm not in work. I'm in town enjoying myself. I hope you have a good day too.' No sooner had I sent the text when my phone rang.

'Hi. Ver you are? I am in town too.' The words were spoken in her deep accent.

'I'm in Eason's bookshop on O'Connell Street; do you know it?' I said.

'Yah, I do. Stay der; I vill come to you.'

'OK, I'm near the side door. I'll see you soon.'

A few minutes later, I saw Maria walk through the door. I became blissfully unaware of everything else going on around me the second she came into view. She greeted me with a great big smile.

'Hi, how arreh you? It nice to see you today.'

'I'm grand. It's great to see you too; it's a nice surprise,' I said.

'Ver you go afterh hereh? I vill come?'

'Well, I haven't had any lunch yet, so I was thinking of going to a café just across the road to get something to eat,' I answered, meaning Montague's on Middle Abbey Street, just opposite the side door of Eason's.

'Is OK I come?'

'Oh God, of course. That would be really nice,' I replied.

A few minutes later, we were sitting in the café at a table by the window. By this point, my stomach was rumbling with the hunger. I ordered a chicken salad sandwich and tea. Maria ordered a coffee. Ten minutes into our conversation, my sandwich arrived looking substantially bigger than I had imagined or wanted it to be. The drinks arrived as well. I was so hungry, I really wanted to eat the sandwich, but I struggled to get my mouth around it with any sense of grace, and then panicked that I would have bits of food caught between my teeth. After eating less than half, I put the sandwich down on the plate and pushed it away.

'Eat yo-rh foodeh,' Maria said in an almost disciplinary tone.

'I'm grand now; I'm not hungry any more.'

'Vy you not hungry now? Go on, eat yo-rh foodeh!'

'No, honestly; I'm good. I've had enough.'

I looked at the sandwich, desperately wanting to pick it up and go for round two, but the thought of her watching me while

I struggled to eat it put me off. We chatted on, and when we had finished our drinks she said she wanted to go to the park to feed the birds. I wondered what park she was talking about, and it soon became apparent that she meant St Stephen's Green. She wanted to feed the ducks.

We got to the Green and headed for the pond. We walked around the park until she found a spot that she liked. She took a plastic bag from her backpack, placed it on the ground and motioned for me to sit on it. She then took out two apples and offered one to me. Once again losing awareness of the rest of the world, I held out my hand to take the apple. 'Wow,' I thought. 'This woman is amazing!' She was growing more and more attractive to me by the minute.

She delved into her bag again. This time she pulled out some bread, which we broke into bits and tossed into the water for the ducks, chatting all the while. When the bread was gone, we walked around the Green, talking as if we had known each other for years. We talked about ourselves and our families and, before we knew it, two and a half hours had passed. I was conscious of the time, as I had arranged to meet a friend. What bloody bad timing! Of all the nights to have to run off! All I wanted to do was stay with Maria and keep chatting.

Maria said she would like to visit the coast on the south side of Dublin, as she hadn't been anywhere other than the north side. I told her Killiney Beach was lovely for a walk and that the Dart trip down was really nice. I volunteered to bring her there sometime if she wanted. Maria quickly said yes.

'Maybe tomorroh we go after work?' she asked.

'Yes, that'd be really nice. Hopefully it will be sunny. If it's raining, we should leave it for another day. I'll ring you tomorrow and we can decide then if we will go.'

'OK goodeh. I hope de sun shine tomorroh.'

'Oh, so do I.'

It was time for me to go. We hugged warmly and, as I let go, my heart was racing. 'Oh my God, what a woman! She's gorgeous,' I thought. As I walked away, I glanced back and saw she was still standing looking after me. She waved. I waved back and smiled and hoped to God that the weather the next day would be spectacular.

Halleluiah! It was a beautiful day; it was June after all. I rang Maria and we arranged to meet at 6 p.m. in front of Clerys on O'Connell Street, under the clock. The place where we had first met when I took her to Swimmin Wimmin. As I headed to Clerys, my stomach was flip-flopping in anticipation of seeing her again. As I got closer, I could see her waiting, looking lovely. We greeted each other with hugs, and the smile I was wearing wasn't going anywhere.

We chatted as we headed for the Dart at Tara Street. We got on the Dart and enjoyed the conversation and the view on the 30-minute trip to Killiney. Getting off the train, we headed for the beach. When we reached the sand, we turned left and walked for five minutes or so till we came to a set of rocks. We found the most comfortable flat ones and sat down. What a setting: sea gently breaking on the shore, sun, and a beautiful woman. 'It doesn't get much better than this,' I thought to myself.

We'd been chatting for about half an hour when Maria said, 'Guess vot I haf in my bag.' With that, she picked up her backpack and began to unzip it.

'I have no idea what you have in your bag,' I said, wondering what she was going to produce from it this time. Her hand disappeared inside and came out with two filled rolls for us to eat. 'Oh, wow! Wonderful,' I grinned, although I was momentarily thrown back to Montague's Café and the problem of how to get my mouth around something so big with any sense of decorum. But then I realised Maria had one as well, so we were both in the same boat. We had just finished off the rolls when Maria said, 'Guess vot else I haf in my bag?'

'Maria, I can't even begin to imagine what else you have in your bag.' She reached into the bag and pulled out two wine glasses, a corkscrew and a bottle of white wine.

'Charah-donnay. Yo-rh fay-vorh-it!' – a fact she had learned in the course of our long and rambling conversation the previous evening. She also took out a bar of dark chocolate.

'Swiss! My fay-vorh-it!' she exclaimed. I was suddenly struck by a strong urge to kiss her. She must have sensed something because she asked, 'Vot you thinking?'

'I'm thinking I'd really love to kiss you, right now.'

'Oh, OK,' she said, which I took to mean, 'OK, kiss me', so I lunged forward. With racing heart and absolute lust, I kissed her, and she responded. We were both unaware of passers-by, and we did not care who saw us. No one was going to interrupt our moment. We surfaced after about ten minutes. My head was spinning, and I couldn't believe this was happening to me.

After spending some hours on the rocks chatting and laughing, with the wine long finished and the light fading, we decided to head back to the Dart. We walked up the beach hand in hand, Maria on my left, beside the water. Just before we left the water's edge, Maria tightened her grip on my hand, pulled me into a firm embrace and kissed me passionately on the lips. I don't know how long it lasted, as time seemed to stand still. Just as suddenly, she pulled her lips away from mine, but still holding me close and fixing her eyes on mine, she said in her oh-so-deep sexy tones, 'Fro-meh Rhussia with love!'

I don't know how I managed to get back across the sand and up to the station; I had quite literally gone weak at the knees, but I got there. We rode back into town on the Dart saying little, gazing into each other's eyes with an unspoken understanding that our next date was going to end up far from a beach.

Noeleen

Going Solo

On a cold January night in 2007, I did two things that changed my life. The first was joining a lesbian soccer team. That led to an explosion of my circle of friends and, through the club, I travelled to Antwerp and Barcelona for EuroGames competitions. The second was booking a lesbian cruise.

A couple of years previously, I went through something that many lesbians experience – the break-up of a long-term relationship. The break-up left me devastated. I had never felt heartache like it before. To blot the pain out and distract myself, I jumped into the Dublin gay scene. I dated a few women who messed me around, but at a lesbian nightclub one night I met Anna. She was quite a bit younger than me, but we clicked and quickly fell for each other. Our relationship was great for a while, but after about a year, the road became more and more rocky due to her shame at being gay and her family pressure to meet a 'nice boy'. Before I knew it, my confidence and pride were being chipped away. The relationship ended and restarted many times, and I found myself longing for something to take my mind off things. An adventure beckoned.

One evening, as I flicked through the pages of the *Gay Community News*, I found myself being drawn to an advert for lesbian cruises. At first I told myself that such trips were for the rich. But the more I thought it over, the more I started to convince myself that this was exactly what I needed. Before I knew it, the deposit for my trip to the Mexican Riviera was put on my credit card and the date was set: 18 October 2007.

The start date for the cruise was a few days before my thirty-first birthday. Once booked, I thought little of it for a few months. But during that summer and in the lead-up to the trip, all I could feel was regret about my decision. I even enquired with the travel company about the cancellation fees. Fear took over, and I had many sleepless nights. However, I told myself that I had spent a whole lot of money on booking this holiday so I had better stop thinking about it and get on the ship.

The aeroplane journey over to the States was uneventful. I remember having a stopover in New York for a couple of hours and the immense feeling of being lost and alone. But when the plane landed in San Diego, where I was to board the cruise ship, excitement came over me. I felt ultimate freedom. Suddenly, this adventure felt very real.

The night before my voyage was due to begin I booked into a hotel close to the port. As soon as I walked into the hotel lobby, a sign caught my eye. It wished ladies about to embark on the Olivia cruise the following day a pleasant trip. Those words excited me. When I reached the floor of my hotel room another sign greeted me. It read, 'Olivia Cruise: Get to Know Your Party – This Way.' As I turned the corner along the corridor of my hotel room, I heard women laughing and American accents. I rushed into my room and locked the door. I just didn't have the courage to go to that party. And then a thought overwhelmed me: if I didn't have the courage to go to that party, how on earth could I get on a ship with 1,800 women? Despite being tired from my journey, I didn't sleep much that night.

The next morning I showered and dressed and had breakfast alone on a wall near some office blocks around the corner from the hotel. As I sat in the sun, I thought how nice downtown San Diego looked. Suddenly Anna popped into my head. I missed her smile. I was daydreaming like a schoolchild, but then realised that the ship would be leaving soon. When I arrived back at the hotel, I remember seeing a line of women queuing for taxis. I grabbed my suitcase from my room, checked out in a panic, and nervously joined the back of the taxi queue. It was obvious that this entire line of excitable women had the same destination ahead – the Olivia cruise ship.

The queue moved quickly, and soon I found myself sharing a taxi with a lovely lesbian couple from the Midwest of America. They were quite interested in the story of how a solo Irish girl had ended up so far away from home. Their warmth and sense of humour helped me to relax until we arrived at the port and joined the enormous queue for the ship itself. Standing in that queue, I remember feeling very young compared to the ladies around me. I kid you not when I say that one lady had a tube coming out of her nose and looked deathly. She could barely walk unassisted. It may sound very shallow, but I started to wonder whether I had picked the right type of holiday. Inside I was freaking out that I might not have anyone my own age to talk to for the next seven days.

Eventually the lines started moving and, as I checked in, the Olivia representative asked whether I was single and, as I was, whether I wanted to sign up for their 'solos' group. She explained that this would involve wearing a dog tag (something I had only seen before in American army movies). The idea was that these would help the single travellers identify each other more easily and that, by wearing it, I could attend solo events such as dinners, breakfasts and special parties. I agreed to it, but couldn't help feeling that the word 'solo' was just a nicer word for 'loser'.

The ship itself was bigger than I could have dreamed: massive elevators to take guests from floor to floor, two large swimming pools, and huge dining areas with all-you-can-eat buffets. Everything was big and bold; everything but my cabin. Although the cost of this trip was more than anything I had spent before on a holiday, I picked a cabin that was within my means, and this of course meant I had to sleep in a room the size of a wardrobe. It also meant that I had to share with a complete stranger.

That stranger was Molly from Seattle. Finally, someone my age! I had been given her profile by the travel agency and was relieved to think I might have a buddy and that hopefully I would not have to spend the next few days alone. Within minutes of starting to unpack, Molly arrived at the door. She was fresh-faced, smiley and warm, and not shy about introducing herself. We were getting on like a house on fire already. I remember us both noticing that we had curtains in the room and saying to each other that we must have a window with a view after all. But when we pulled back the curtains, we fell around laughing when we discovered that behind the curtains was a wall. They were just there for decoration. I liked her sense of humour, and I had a feeling that the trip was going to be OK.

The solos dog tag turned out to be a great idea. Soon I realised that a group of singletons between the ages of twenty to forty existed on board, all travelling alone and all in need of this trip for one reason or another. My fears of being alone dissipated.

Daytime on the ship was fun. Quickly I got into a routine of meeting the solo ladies for breakfast and, after gorging on the amazing food, we would head towards the deck for afternoon sunbathing and cocktails. I soon befriended two ladies who I initially assumed were a couple but turned out to be far from it. Anita was originally from Ireland but now lived in San Francisco. Her companion was Cecilia, a Mexican woman living in the same city. They had been friends for only a short time, but decided to go on the cruise together as both were hoping to find some romance. It soon came to light that they were both irritating one another, and Anita confessed that she wasn't really enjoying herself. It didn't help that the two were sharing a tiny cabin. It really surprised me that she wasn't enjoying this amazing experience at sea.

Because of our Irish connection, Anita and I became close. We would sit by the bar on deck with some beers and open our hearts to one another. Well, in reality, she would talk a lot about heartache and her history, and I would lend her a sympathetic ear.

It was Cecilia, however, who changed how I saw myself. Each night at dinner, I found myself being watched by her. She was keen to get my attention, and I felt like the most important person on the entire ship when I was around her. Cecilia was butch, confident and in her late forties. It was soon obvious to me that she was desperate to land herself a younger woman whom she could spoil. Her flirtations were initially overpowering, but soon I wallowed in her attention towards me. At times I felt a bit cruel as, although I wasn't physically attracted to this woman, I enjoyed her company. I felt my confidence improve with each moment we spent together. When she looked at me, it was as if she was looking at a diamond. I had never felt this way before, and I liked it.

The days and nights on the ship passed along at a nice pace. I enjoyed going on excursions around the Mexican ports. As Cecilia knew the language, our small group of solos felt safer exploring the local towns in her company. She seemed so strong and unfazed. But then one night, something silly happened on the ship. I kissed her! It came out of the blue and took us both by surprise. I knew straight away that I had crossed a line. I had no desire to go any further with it. I liked being around her because she made me feel good about myself, but I didn't want to confuse things. I found myself avoiding her for the next couple of days and, when we did speak, I avoided speaking about our encounter.

Thankfully, Cecilia was mature and wise enough to understand. She backed off and diverted her attention towards another woman. By the end of the holiday, we were close buddies again. She made a huge effort on the night of my birthday, and we spent the last few days on the ship hanging out.

Before I knew it, the holiday was coming to an end, and it was time to say goodbye to one another. I felt the dread of knowing that soon I would be back in Ireland, thousands of miles away from these fantastic people. I didn't want this adventure to end, but of course it had to.

When I look back now on that holiday, I realise how the journey changed me. I began to see my tumultuous relationship with Anna with different eyes. By the time I returned home, I had regained my lost confidence. Most important, however, was that I had had ten days of fun and indulgence. Through the connections I made on that cruise, I ended up living in San Francisco for a year. But that's another story.

Natalie Dunne

Happy Coming Out

I had only been seeing my lovely ex for a week when I started coming out. First, I told my sister Nora, whose response was, 'About bloody time!' The rest of my family had similar wonderful reactions, like my mother's 'When can we meet her?'

I rang my sister Kathryn, who lives in England, and told her over the phone. She was happy for me, but I thought there was a bit of excitement or congratulations missing from her voice. I guess I couldn't have expected everyone to be as excited as me.

But I got a great laugh one week later when a card arrived for me in the post (yes, these were pre-internet days). It was a 'happy-coming-out' card from Kathryn. I didn't even know such cards existed. The image on the card was a very unbecoming picture of a drag queen in pink gingham. They obviously have a better variety of cards in England! Coming-out cards are only just appearing here now. I thought it was brilliant, funny and tacky, and I was delighted that Kathryn could make fun of it all.

I was then, and am now, an avid recycler, so I always kept any good cards I received to reuse or to pass on to others. These included very beautiful, arty, sexy, funny or unusual cards. Kathryn's coming-out card definitely fell into this category.

Occasionally, I'd come across it and wonder when or with whom I would get the chance to reuse it. You can imagine then my surprise, and indeed Kathryn's, when fifteen years later she told me she was in a relationship with a woman. Yes, she received the same well-kept, drag-queen-in-pink-gingham card herself.

Breege Fahy

Hindsight

My childhood was unremarkable, in the sense that no major good or bad things happened to me. There was nothing that pushed me in one direction or another. Everything was average, normal. At least, that is how it was on the surface, but it was not how I felt inside. I felt anything but normal. I was not sure what about me was different, but I knew something was. I played with Sindy and Barbie like lots of other girls, but my Barbie didn't have a Ken; she was a single mother whose best friend was Sindy. This was odd since, as a child, I did not know any single mothers; I did not know any children with no father figures at home.

At the time, my best friend was a girl named Rebecca. She was my first friend and, as far as I was concerned, I had dibs on her. I was far from happy when an elderly couple on our street had their granddaughter come to stay with them for a few months. Her name was Denise, and most of the time she lived in China with her parents. This made her exotic to the likes of us, who weren't allowed to cross the road without adult supervision. Denise had set her sights on Rebecca and wanted to be her best friend. And, as every eight-year-old girl knows, you can only have one best friend.

I was hugely jealous one summer's day when I looked out my bedroom window and saw Rebecca and Denise walking towards Rebecca's house. I stared at them with such intensity that I was sure I could will Rebecca to turn on her heel and head towards my house instead. It didn't happen, and suddenly they were out of view. I ran downstairs, out the front door, through my garden, up the road and around the corner. I crept on my hunkers along the path until I reached the hedge surrounding Rebecca's house. Peeping over, I saw the front door close behind Denise. I returned to my room to sit by my window and wait for Denise to walk back across the green to her house, which I had full view of. Every few minutes, I would sneak into my parents' room and peep out their window, from which I could see into Rebecca's bedroom. I was filled with not only intense jealousy and anger that another girl was getting to spend time with Rebecca, but also a growing confusion. I knew there was something not quite 'normal' about the intensity of my feelings for Rebecca.

These days, like the rest of the civilised world, I only stalk women on Facebook; otherwise, I'd surely have a few restraining orders on me by now. Still, throughout my childhood, I was plagued by strange feelings and actions that I couldn't explain. I had no crushes on boys like the other girls. On one occasion, when grilled by a classmate about what boy I fancied, I felt the need to make one up just so they would leave me alone. I blurted out the first boy's name I could think of – my brother's name, Mark. Lucky for me there was a Mark amongst the group of boys that my classmate knew and, apparently, he was way out of my league, so they never bothered to try getting us together. I was so relieved. I felt as if I had stopped them from finding out my secret. I actually had no idea what my secret was, but I knew I had one, and the thought of it being discovered made me panic. I had dodged a bullet.

For my thirteenth birthday, my parents brought me, Rebecca and Rebecca's friend Anna to the Chicago Pizza Pie Factory. My folks had said I could bring two friends, but I didn't have two friends. I just had Rebecca. She was a different type of creature to me. She had grown into a pretty, playful and popular teenager, not the moody teen with a temper that everyone knew me to be. She had lots of friends, all of whom I considered to be in the same league as her, a league above my own. And, so, Rebecca suggested bringing her friend Anna. I didn't dislike her as much as I did Denise, probably because she wasn't around as often, so I didn't see her as a threat. Anna had straight, dark-brown hair down to her waist, which was as shiny as freshly waxed cherry oak. She walked with her shoulders back and her chin up, full of quiet confidence. A picture of poise and manners.

I had a disposable camera to capture the day. Even back then I loved taking photos. I would often think, 'When I'm older people will look at these photos and think I was popular.' This somehow comforted me whenever I felt down or confused about my place in the world. Disposable cameras were a new thing, a cheap and easy way to be a real, grown-up photographer. All you had to do was peel off the stiff plastic wrapper and wind the dial on the camera until a number appeared in the tiny hole on the top.

We chatted and joked and studied our menus in the very American surroundings of the restaurant. Our waitress arrived, and I straightaway noticed how pretty she was. Tall and slim, with a pleasant yet slightly shy manner. She asked for our orders and commented on this and that with all the well-rehearsed pleasantries an experienced waitress should have. All of which was done without lifting her eyes to meet any of ours. This pretty red-headed lady walked away from our table with my eyes on her every move and my neck craning to keep her in sight, until she disappeared into the kitchen.

Waiting for her to return with our pizzas felt like an eternity. I fidgeted with my camera, clicking and winding, clicking and winding, as I took photos of the American knick-knacks around us. When the waitress appeared, balancing our plates along her arms, I turned my full attention to her. I took her photo without thinking, and a second photo just to be certain I had captured her face on film.

'Why are you taking photos of the waitress?' my father asked.

My camera and my eyes went straight to the table. A sudden rush of panic, embarrassment and confusion swept over me. Like a wave about to drown me, my mind was flooded with excuses, questions and answers I didn't want to know. The uncensored response came into my mind before I could stop it:

'Because she is so pretty, and I want to remember the soft red curls of her hair, the pinkness of her angular lips and the milky white porcelain of her skin.' I bit my lip hard so as not to blurt out this answer. I had no idea what to say, but I so desperately didn't want that answer to escape from my lips. Eventually, I looked up and realised no one was even looking at me. No one was waiting for an answer. The meal and the conversation had moved on; my father's question had been nothing more than a passing enquiry. Apparently only I had paid it any attention.

Why had this question panicked me so much? I spent the rest of our time in the Chicago Pizza Pie Factory desperately trying to 'act normal', while panic and confusion raced in circles around my mind. Sideward glances at the waitress that I hoped no one would notice just added fuel to my confusion.

Rebecca and I parted ways when we were fourteen, at her request. She explained that we were no longer 'part of the same crowd' and that it would be easier for both of us if we stuck to our own friends. Of course, Rebecca knew she was my only friend, but she would never be so cruel as to say it. It was kinder for her to imply that I had other friends, and I played along willingly. As far as I was concerned, I was lucky to have been her friend for as long as I had been. I always knew a day would come when I'd be discovered to be the odd person out.

At fifteen, I was completely devoid of friends and social experiences. I had never been kissed, and this concerned me greatly since it seemed like every other girl my age had been. Then one day I met Eve in the school canteen and was drawn to her for reasons I couldn't explain. She became my one friend during my teen years. But our friendship was very tough at times; it wasn't your average teen friendship. Eve was weighted down by a guilt that had fermented inside her since a stranger, years before, stole her childhood and left her the shell of the person she could have been.

But to me Eve was beautiful. She was the most talented, intelligent and funny person I had ever met. I relished every second that I got to spend with her, and when I wasn't around her, my thoughts always turned to her.

Because of her past experience, Eve didn't like to be touched. We didn't hug, we didn't exchange childlike cuddles, and we didn't link arms like young teens normally do. One day, in her parents' house, her bare arm brushed against mine. I held my breath without realising it. The hairs on my arm stood up, and a tingle rippled down from my scalp and along my spine to the soles of my feet. The world around me blurred. Eve turned to look at me, not even realising that she had brushed against me. My heart raced and I panicked as everything came back into focus. For a second I knew exactly what I was, even if I didn't have a name for it or if I didn't fully understand it. For that one second it was clear, but without even making a conscious decision to do so, I pushed the thought far out of my mind. And there it stayed till I got to college.

Joanne and I met during our first year of college, when I was eighteen. We became friends along with two other girls, Fran and Beth. The four of us gravitated towards each other and, soon enough, we were inseparable. At the time, I was going from one man to another, thinking that at some point one of them would make me feel what I had heard so many of my friends speak of – the fireworks-in-your-eyes and butterflies-in-your-stomach sensation you're supposed to feel when you're attracted to someone.

Joanne, Fran, Beth and I were having the time of our lives in college. It was the first time I ever felt like I could be myself, relax and have fun. I was going to parties and hanging out with the 'cool gang'. I felt popular, and that was a completely new experience for me. I was drawn to Joanne, but I wasn't quite sure why. There was definitely no physical attraction or intensity like there had been with Eve; it was more of a sisterly thing.

Joanne and I, along with a handful of other students from our course, were drafted in to serve wine at a photography exhibition that our tutor was holding. After hours of the 'one-glass-for-you-and-one-glass-for-me' routine, we ended up more than a little drunk, with the sleeves of our crisp white shirts soaked in red wine. As the last few guests left, Joanne and I sneaked off with a bottle each to the disabled toilet at the back of the building. Through a fit of drunken giggles, I told her that I knew she was gay, explaining that it 'took one to know one'. It was not only the first time I had ever said I was gay out loud, but the first time I had even admitted it to myself. It was as if my mouth had taken over and was spitting out the words before my brain had a chance to stop it. When I realised what I had said and, more important, that Joanne didn't seem to think I was crazy, I suddenly felt a great weight had been lifted. I could finally breathe easy. With those breaths I laughed louder and harder than I ever had before. It was a laugh of nerves, relief and excitement. Over and over in my head I repeated, 'I'm gay. I'm gay.'

Before my giggles had time to die away, Joanne grabbed me by the wrist and declared that she was going to get me my first lesbian kiss that very night. With that, she dragged me off to a dingy gay bar that, before that night, I never knew existed. After a lot of coaxing from Joanne, I was set up with the only available girl in the bar and had my first lesbian kiss, which I can only describe as completely unremarkable. And yet, after talking to Joanne and being in that bar, I realised that I didn't have to force these thoughts from my mind any more. I could let them creep into my conscious, to develop and take shape. I could finally entertain the thought that I wasn't straight, knowing then that I wasn't alone.

Elizabeth-Jane Smyth

I Knew He Knew, but He Didn't Know
I Knew He Knew

I was away from home and only 22 years old when I came out to myself. I was working at a summer camp in the United States for six months, and it was there that I met my first partner, Charna. For years before that, I was in what I now realise was denial. 'No, no, no; I'm not gay!' A few different people had touched on it, and I had wondered once or twice myself, but I knew no other gay people and just presumed I was more of a tomboy. I really enjoyed the company of boys, so in my mind I wasn't a man-hater, and therefore I wasn't a lesbian.

As a teenager, I had a couple of taunts about being gay from my mum and one of my sisters as well. They had laughed and sniggered at the fact that I had never had a boyfriend and asked me if I was a lesbian. That only made me more of the opinion that I wasn't. 'No, I am not!' I insisted. 'I am most definitely not gay!' To be honest, it was probably not so much that I was even suppressing my feelings; I was just trying to insist that I was 'normal', for want of a better word.

So, in 2001, I got the travelling bug and headed to the States to work at a kids' camp. I had a great summer adventure. A trip that changed my life forever! I met Charna and some other openly gay girls and had an absolute whale of a time. Charna and I decided that we were going to try to stay together but, initially, we had to go our separate ways. She was from Australia and I was from England. Charna needed to go back to Australia, as she'd already been travelling for over five years at that point.

I didn't have the money to follow her, so I headed home and started to work to build up some funds for our next chapter. It was hard to be separated from her, but it felt right at the time. The September 11 attacks had also happened around this time. It was a strange period, but it was nice to go home.

We went our separate ways, and we both worked hard for the next four or five months. The following March, Charna came over to the UK. We looked at our options of where we could go next, due to the fact that we both had visa restrictions in the other's home country, and we decided to go to Ireland. We were staying with my dad from March until August, until we moved over to Ireland. The only family member I had told I was gay, however, was my aunt, partly because she is one of my closest family members and also because upon my return from the States she asked whether I had had any holiday romances. In some ways, I wanted to tell my dad, but in other ways I felt that if my sisters didn't feel the need to say, 'Hey, Dad, I'm heterosexual', then why should I have to say, 'Hey, Dad, I'm homosexual'? And I suppose I felt deep down that he would just figure it out and we'd cross that bridge when we came to it.

So we were plodding along and everything was grand. Thankfully, I had a very close relationship with my dad then, and I still do now. He really bonded with Charna when she arrived. In fact, he even joked to me when he first met her that he wished he was twenty years younger, which tickled Charna and me, but also confirmed that he didn't have a clue what was going on between us. Then my aunt, in a roundabout way, took it upon herself to plant the seed for him to figure it out. It wasn't long before he put two and two together. Apparently they had a deep and meaningful conversation about it, and he was grand. But he told my aunt that he wasn't going to mention it as he didn't want to embarrass me. So it got to the point where I knew he knew, but he didn't know I knew he knew. This went on for a little while. It went unsaid. And after living with him for a few months, he began to treat Charna like one of his daughters. He is very loving in that way anyway.

Eventually, Charna and I moved to Ireland. One of my sisters jumped on the bandwagon and decided to move to Ireland as well. A couple of months later, my dad and his partner told us they were coming to visit for the New Year. They literally flew in late in the afternoon on New Year's Eve, and it was a bit of a mad rush to get everyone together and get down to the pub in time for the celebrations. When we eventually did get everyone together, we were all having a lovely time.

At the stroke of midnight, my dad grabbed my sister and gave her a kiss. He then got hold of me with one arm and said, 'Happy New Year,' before grabbing Charna with his other arm. He has always kissed my sisters and me on the forehead due to his prickly beard, so he gave Charna and me each a kiss on the forehead. Then he said, 'I know you know!'

Pleasantly surprised at his choice of timing, I replied, 'I know you know, Dad.'

He then turned to Charna and said, 'You just look after my little girl, and I'll be happy enough with that.'

So that was that. We didn't dwell on it, and we didn't talk about it the next day. I was relieved that he knew I knew and I knew that he knew, and everything was just fine. Happy days!

Over the last ten years, we've never really discussed my being gay, but it is lovely to know that he is fine with it. There have been times when I thought that maybe it would come up or maybe there would be a bit of awkwardness between us. When Charna and I went our separate ways, for example, I didn't quite know how he would take it or whether he'd raise any questions. But thankfully he has always been cool with all of my partners, not that there have been that many!

One of the funny stories about my dad and me involves the fact that we are both into motorbikes. On one occasion, he came to visit me in Ireland by himself. We were going to a Harley rally, and we were riding through Waterford city. We had to slow down whilst driving along the quays and, out of the corner of my eye, I saw three good-looking girls walking by. I just happened to turn to have a little look at them and, at the same time, I noticed that my dad had turned to have a little look at them as well. We each copped that the other was looking at the girls, and we just had the biggest smiles on our faces. Then my dad said, 'I can't believe my daughter is checking out the same girls as I am!'

And I said, 'You can't believe it? I can't believe that you are checking them out when you're old enough to be their dad!' So we had one of those moments and then just rode off.

I had a nice 'coming out', really. I did not want it to be a big drama, and it hasn't been a drama. I strongly believe that if you make something a drama then everybody else will make it a drama as well. I didn't feel that I had to have a major coming out to anyone.

It has been a slightly different story with my mum. I've never discussed the fact that I'm gay with my mum, and I probably never will, as we are not close. She told my sisters that she thought it was just a 'phase' I was going through. So if that's what she thinks, then so be it. But it's been a bloody long phase! It's sad, but I am very lucky to have a different relationship with my dad. At least I have that relationship with one parent. Some people don't have it with either, so I am fortunate in that sense.

Sadly, and regretfully, I never told my nan, even though we were very close. A couple of years ago, we were in the States together at my aforementioned aunt's house, and my aunt had 'the conversation' with my nan. And, yet again, I knew that she knew and vice versa, but we never spoke about it.

One day I was on Skype with Ania, a girl I was kind of seeing, and Nan walked into the room. 'Oh, is that your close friend?' she asked. I said it was. Nan was baffled by the whole Skype thing and was more confused about how we could see each other. Bless her! She just waved and said a big 'Hello, Ania!' and walked away chuckling to herself and muttering something about modern technology.

Later that evening, the two of us went out for dinner. 'You know, Laura,' she said, 'I'm very open-minded, and if there's ever anything you need to talk about, then I'm here for you.' I knew exactly what she was referring to, but we both knew she didn't need to push it any more. There was nothing I needed to say. If there had been, then I knew I could have said something.

All I said in return was, 'I know you are, Nan. And don't worry; if there is ever anything, then I know I can talk to you.' But I didn't need to talk about anything then. There was nothing major going on at that point in time and nothing I needed her support with. Very sadly, she died unexpectedly soon after that incident, and that's why I regret not having had a proper conversation with her. Maybe she had questions, and now I'll never know. However, it is very nice to know that she appeared to be perfectly OK with the situation. Over the years, my sisters would bring boyfriends to her home and I would bring 'friends'. I suppose deep down she had probably known for quite some time.

I've always known that Dad and Nan felt that if we were happy, they were happy. That's a nice quality to have. My sisters are cool about it as well. Regretfully, I didn't tell one of my sisters myself, and she found out through my other sister. She felt hurt that maybe I didn't trust her. Initially, she commented, 'I don't think you are.' She seemed to struggle with it a little bit, not really understanding. She got over it, though, and is fine now. Overall, I'm very fortunate with how my family and friends have accepted me for who I am. And for those that don't, it's their loss!

Laura

Inside Out

'It's just a phase,' I remember telling myself. I had been married for nine years, I had two kids, and I was in the middle of a fairly traumatic separation when I found myself having my first ever lesbian relationship. Sure, I couldn't possibly be gay. I remember being angry at God, thinking, 'Look, I have enough to deal with already. Why do you have to make me gay on top of all this?' I mean, I was 35. Surely you couldn't turn gay at 35, and after having two children! Well, one thing for certain was that I couldn't! I had two children to think about, and no way could I be a gay mother. I couldn't do that to my children. I told myself it was just a phase, and when the relationship ended I swept the whole thing under the carpet, never to be thought about again.

Time moved on, and I worked on building myself up from the inside out. I hadn't realised how lost I had been in my marriage; I had to find 'me' again. As I worked through the process of finding myself, I became close to another friend. Our friendship grew closer and more meaningful, and I found myself in yet another lesbian relationship. 'This can't be happening,' I thought. 'This is not me!' But it was; this was exactly who I was … a lesbian. I didn't want to believe it. I couldn't accept it. This had to be another phase. But it wasn't. My feelings grew stronger for this other woman, and I knew deep down that it was something I was actually going to have to face within myself. Can you imagine how scary that was?

The relationship ended, and I was very upset. I knew then that it was not just a phase; it was part of who I am. 'I must be bisexual,' I reasoned. 'I can't be gay; I'm bisexual!' For the next few years I worked on learning to accept that, and I knew one day that I would have to face up to telling my children. Now that was a scary thought!

My first step to acceptance, as I thought, was to tell someone. I needed people to talk to, so I decided to tell my friends. The build up to it was something that I had never experienced before; my heart was fluttering, and my nerves were shot. The anxiety was overwhelming. I still wasn't even sure whether I was gay at all. There's nothing like denial and fear to stop you looking at something that's staring you straight (or should I say gay) in the face. I guess the only way I could handle something so big and scary was to let it in just one little bit at a time.

The only label that came close to describing how I felt then was 'bisexual'. Even though I knew deep down I was just gay, it was too big of a step to take all in one go. The opportunity arose for me to tell some friends, and I blurted it out. 'I've had a relationship with a woman, and I don't know what that means. I must be gay … I can't be … I don't know. HELP!'

I didn't expect what was about to unfold. I mean, my friends were going to think I was such a fraud and that I had been lying to them all this time. But their reaction was fantastic. There was me expecting shock and horror, but it didn't come. I was actually shocked at the lack of shock and almost disappointed in a weird way. I remember one of my friends saying, 'Look, it's OK. You are still the same great person to me that you have always been.' I can't describe in words how much it meant for me to hear that at the time. It even makes me cry now as I write this. So I wasn't a total fraud after all. I was still me. My friends still liked me. There was hope after all. What a relief!

Next stop … I had to tell my sisters. We were heading away on a weekend together, and it felt like the right time to tell them. I thought, 'Ah sure they'll have all weekend to ask me questions about it; it will be fine.' So there I was telling them: 'I may be gay, I may be straight; I'm very confused and upset. I have no idea how all of this is going to affect the kids. All I want to do is tell you that right now I'm upset. I don't know what to do, but what I want from you is to support me and to be happy for me.' But it wasn't fine. I was looking for the same great reaction I had received from my friends, and when I didn't get that, I didn't want to know. I didn't really talk to my sisters much about it afterwards.

Well, not until we went away on holidays again. I had been feeling the tension between us and I knew that something was going to give at some point and the row that had been brewing for months finally exploded. It wasn't pretty and I swore in my head at the time never to talk to them again. Which actually only lasted until the next morning when we cleared the air once and for all.

I came to understand that when people who are close to you, especially family, see that you're upset, it's actually unrealistic to expect them to be happy for you. I also realised that they are entitled to have their own reaction and to take some time to get used to the idea. I mean, look at the reaction I had myself: denial, non-acceptance, upset, hate, anger, confusion, rejection, etc. So expecting my sisters to be happy for me straight away, when I wasn't happy with myself after a few years of coming to terms with it, was unfair of me. It was unfair to have only expected and allowed for a happy, supportive reaction when I couldn't be happy or supportive myself. It was like I was screaming out to my sisters, 'Please accept me', and it was only then that the penny finally dropped and I realised that I had to accept myself first.

So I continued to work on myself from the inside out, and I found myself in a place where I was genuinely ready for a relationship again. I was ready to say yes to love, I was ready to say yes to being gay, I was ready to say yes to being me, and I was going to build on being ready to tell the kids at some point in the future. Well, lucky for me, love came knocking on my door, and I said, 'Yes! Come on in, because I'm coming out!' I haven't looked back since.

I have met the most beautiful, caring, loving, understanding, thoughtful girlfriend anyone could ask for. I have never been as happy in myself or in a relationship as I am right now.

I have been on the road to self-acceptance ever since, and what a difference that has made. I have found myself truly at home, truly happy and enjoying every minute that being a lesbian has to offer. All I can say is that I love being a lesbian. Imagine that! After all the trauma I put myself through, it turns out that I love being a lesbian. I wonder, as I look back now, why on earth I fought myself so hard on it in the first place, when freedom is always to be found in self-acceptance. And now that I'm out the other end it just seems so ridiculous, because the homophobe I expected to meet outside me only ever existed in my own mind. It was always only me getting in my own way. In a way, that was the biggest shock of all.

Next stop was to finally tell my kids. The right time was getting closer and closer by the day. It wasn't a matter of 'if' any more but 'when'. It felt pretty scary.

I had finally found another mother to talk to, a mother like me who had already told her kids. It turned out that I wasn't the only gay mother in the world after all! The best advice she gave me was to be as open as possible about my relationship so that when it came time to actually tell my kids, I would only be confirming something they already knew. For example, she said to tell them when my girlfriend and I were going out to dinner, to tell them when I was going to visit her, to show them any presents she gave me, and even for all of us to go on holiday together. Little things like that to give them enough clues to figure it out in their own way.

So we worked away like that for a while, and I was getting a little bit braver and a little bit more honest every day, until finally I felt the time was right for me and for them. I knew from my experiences so far, and from advice that I had gotten, that it was very important to convey the message that I was happy, and also that I had a genuine spirit of self-acceptance about it. I was confident by then that I felt both of those. I was no longer confused and upset, and I had also learned that it was important to allow for whatever reaction came my way.

Now, I'm not going to lie to you, even with everything I had learned so far, and the happy place I was in, it was not an easy thing to do. My plan to give them enough clues to figure it out had worked perfectly, because as soon as I mentioned what I wanted to talk about, they already knew what I was going to say. So while that part was easy, watching the tears roll down the cheeks of my fourteen-year-old daughter was heartbreaking to say the least. It did help that my nineteen-year-old seemed OK about it. I remember feeling totally exposed and vulnerable afterwards, knowing it was not something I could ever unsay or take back. I had got the reactions I was expecting, considering the ages of the kids, but the thing that took me by surprise was that, even though I had spent all those years building up to that moment, looking forward to finally crossing the end of the line, so to speak, I discovered that I was actually at the beginning of something else. And that beginning consisted of three other people as well as me. So instead of thinking, 'Yippee; it's all over with now', though I did feel that way a bit, I had a stronger feeling that there was still another mountain or two to cross.

Ever since then, we have been crossing those mountains with lots of small baby steps, getting further along the path every day. My then nineteen-year-old's unbelievably fantastic reaction still leaves me speechless to this day. And after three years of waiting for some sort of explosion from her, there is absolutely no sign of it coming. In fact, telling her changed how she related to my girlfriend. She went from being distant to being so much more welcoming and friendly, to the point that they now dance at family Christmas parties without me. On the other hand, my then fourteen-year-old went from being friendly to being distant with my girlfriend and me. It has not been an easy thing for any of us to manage, but things get better every day, and we have come a long way from where we were.

After telling the kids, I found myself going through a phase of non-acceptance again in terms of being a gay mother. I was making the gay part of me so big that I couldn't find the right balance of being a mother, which led to me being too easy as a mother. So I worked on accepting myself as a gay mother, making the gay part of me smaller, so to speak, and remembering that it is OK to be gay and a mother at the same time. This has helped me to accept that I am still the best mother I can be, regardless of my sexuality. I have also learned that to help my younger daughter to be OK and to feel better about it all, I had to learn to be OK first, just as with my sisters. I have worked on learning to be confident around her in relation to being gay, and the more confident I feel, the more improvements I notice in her. I know she has even told some of her friends, which I think is quite amazing for a now sixteen-year-old. She still sometimes drifts between being distant and friendly with my girlfriend, but another thing I have had to learn is to step back and let them figure out their relationship for themselves. I did try to stay on the middle ground for a while, but that was just so much pressure on me. I was feeling torn, trying to keep everyone happy, and only ever keeping one person happy, at the other person's expense. So I have had to step back from that no-win situation, because I need to look after myself too.

As you can see, it continues to be a learning curve. There is no road map and no set of instructions to follow, but we are all working at it in our own ways. I can't thank my girlfriend enough for being so patient and understanding. The greatest birthday present she gave me last year was to organise for the kids to come out to dinner as a surprise. The message was loud and clear that night: they all love me and accept me for me, regardless of whatever is happening.

This is an ongoing journey that has been challenging at times, and no doubt there will be more challenges to face. But being true to me has been so much easier and so much better for me and everybody in my life, including my kids, than pretending I was somebody else. At the end of the day, we get one life and, as one of my favourite songs says, 'I hope you dance!'

My hope for anyone reading this is that you find the courage to be yourself.

Leanne

I Travelled Across the World
to Find Myself and My Home

I always knew that there was something different about me, but I had no idea what it was. My mother was a model in Italy; she had her own fashion label and was the epitome of femininity. For as long as I remember, I tried my best to fit the mould of the perfect daughter she had imagined for me, but it wasn't long before the reality of who I was shattered that mould and out of it emerged the person I was always meant to be.

My journey started in Italy as I was born in Rome to Sri Lankan parents. When I was twelve, my parents' marriage began to crumble and they began a trial separation. My mother stayed in Italy to mind the family business she had started, a chain of fashion boutiques, and my father and I moved back to Sri Lanka. I moved in with my grandparents and my father began his own garment business. At this point, both my parents lost sight of me as they were too busy rebuilding their respective lives.

As a child I had very little time for dolls; instead I craved all the toys in the boys' section – Dinky cars, remote-control cars, robots and transformers. Prior to my teens, my parents reluctantly gave into my tantrums and stopped buying me dolls, as they genuinely thought it was just a phase. Little did they know!

Being a teenager was very challenging for me. Not only did I move country, learn a new language, adapt to a new culture and weather my parents' long, tumultuous separation, we also changed religion! My mother, who had been very liberal, became a fanatical Jehovah's Witness overnight, and although my father was now in another relationship, he too embraced the new religion. Looking back now, I think my parents were very unhappy individuals who looked for solace in religion. Suddenly, I was no longer allowed to have friends from outside the 'faith'. I had to attend five bible-study meetings a week and go preaching. I remember thinking that my life was officially over. Just at that point, unlike my girlfriends who were lusting after Duran Duran and Wham!, I became totally besotted with Madonna. My walls were covered from floor to ceiling with provocative images of the Pop Queen. I remember quite regularly my mother would rip her posters off my wall, calling her 'the Antichrist'. Each time, I would defiantly put them back up the following day. The reason for my devotion to Madonna, which has now lasted over twenty years, was that she made me believe I could be something other than what was expected of me. She was the first woman who made me start questioning my sexuality.

The first time I kissed a girl I was sixteen. Her name was Lina. She was an Italian Jehovah's Witness. My mother ran a chain of boutiques, and every summer she would take part in an international fashion fair in Palermo in Sicily. The very morning the fair was due to open, my mother fell down some stairs and broke both her feet. Lina was hired to help me manage the stand in her absence. It was a very intense two weeks. There was this insane chemistry between us. At the end of the fair, Lina offered to show me the sights of Palermo and took me to see Monte Pellegrino. That's where it happened. Fireworks went off inside me and everything became clear. I thought, 'This is it! This is what my life is all about.' Everything I had been struggling with, feeling like I didn't fit in, and my crush on Madonna, it all made sense in this one amazing moment.

All that summer we were at it like rabbits, and my mother didn't have a clue because she couldn't climb the stairs! As we lay out on the balcony in the open air under the stars, I did half-expect a bolt of lightning from God to hit us, but maybe the

Jehovah's Witness God took pity on me and thought I deserved a break.

That summer shaped the rest of my life. A few months later I was back in Sri Lanka, and when my parents found out I was gay I was kicked out of my grandparents' house. I was just seventeen years old.

The next few years are a bit hazy. I can't remember much about them except that I bummed around a lot and stayed with friends and lovers. I got a job in radio and TV, but I knew my career would be held back because of my sexuality. Those years were incredibly hard for me. I felt abandoned and completely alone. I found life in Sri Lanka very challenging and unkind, so I decided to emigrate. At the age of 21, I joined a Middle Eastern airline as a flight attendant based in Bahrain.

Working as a flight attendant was a blast. I got to see the world, stayed in five-star hotels and, most important, for the first time I started questioning who I wanted to be in this world. After five years, I was considering emigrating once again, to either Australia or Ireland. I had my place booked in a Melbourne university but, at the very last minute, I changed my mind and decided to go to Ireland, partly because I liked the idea of returning to Europe, but mostly because I genuinely liked the Irish.

I finally arrived in Ireland in June 2000. I was just 25 years old. I had IR£1,250 in my pocket, I knew only one person, and I had no idea what I was going to do with myself. However, I knew two things for sure: first, I wanted to live in a country that accepted me for who I was, even though at that time I had no clue what that was and, second, I knew I had this relentless fire in my belly that would often keep me up at night and that made me believe I had a lot to offer this world but, again, I had no idea what shape that would take. I was ready to work hard and give living in Ireland my best shot.

Like many migrants, I started from the very bottom and worked my way up. I worked as a kitchen porter, catering assistant, bartender, waitress, receptionist, HR administrator, junior recruitment consultant, senior recruitment consultant, to finally owning my own training company in 2006.

Then that same year I noticed how the face of Irish media was not changing to reflect our New Ireland. Media was my first love back in Sri Lanka, so I started to volunteer in a community radio station in Blanchardstown, where I produced and presented a live radio show. This then led me to join the Newstalk team in 2008 to present *Global Village*, a social justice and mental health programme that airs every Saturday at 7 p.m. The programme has won a number of awards and still remains the only one of its kind in mainstream Irish media.

In my travels in both the media and corporate worlds, I began to notice the lack of visibility of lesbians. There were plenty of gay men but no lesbians. I couldn't understand this, and after numerous conversations with other lesbians I came to one conclusion: lesbians were not visible in Irish society due to a lack of role models, and low levels of confidence due to the absence of family supports and a sense of community. As a result, many lesbians have been unable to participate fully and reach their true potential both within the LGBTQ community and wider Irish society.

Then I remembered my first experience of 'coming out' and being in a gay space. It was the Candy Bar in Soho in London. I was 23 years old. My sheltered upbringing made the idea of stepping into a gay space where I was going to meet another lesbian for the first time in my life quite simply terrifying for me. Sure enough, what I saw was more than I could handle at the time – butch, femme, suits, ties, leather, chains, shaved heads, torn T-shirts, studs, tattoos, piercings ... my brain was struggling to take it all in. I remember being anxious as I asked myself again the questions that were haunting me for so many years: Is this really me? Am I really a lesbian? It was a brand new world for me, and I felt very far from proud. I was frightened and confused, and I felt painfully inadequate.

Most members of our community have similar stories of when they first came out, as we didn't have any alternative. Many of us overcame our initial nerves and awkwardness by sheer brute force, often fuelled by alcohol and drugs, which sometimes led to a multitude of other issues, such as addiction and STDs.

Imagine for a minute if your first experience of the LGBTQ community was in a safe, nurturing and supportive environment, an environment where you would have an opportunity to explore your sexuality, become self-aware and connect with other women who have just started their own journeys of self-discovery.

In 2011 my partner, Anne Marie Toole, a qualified psychotherapist, and I co-founded Insight Matters, a mental health support service. It was our vision to create a space that provides personal development, counselling and psychotherapy services to the LGBTQ community. Many LGBTQ people are marginalised and isolated from their family and community through the 'coming-out' process, which is often the culmination of many years of soul-searching and great pain. This frequently results in leaving school early and working in low-paid jobs, which can lead to a huge lack of confidence and personal well-being. This often manifests itself in alcohol and drug abuse and a lack of opportunities. Lesbians face unique barriers within both the LGBTQ and wider communities, and our services are designed with their needs in mind.

I came to Ireland fifteen years ago, and I can honestly say that Ireland has been good to me. Not only have I reaped many benefits professionally but I have also, for the first time, found happiness in my personal life. I feel comfortable in my own skin, and I have found true love in a beautiful Irish woman named Anne Marie. I am even engaged! However, the best moment so far was on 25 November 2014, when my beloved partner Anne Marie and I shared the wonderful news that I am pregnant. It took us two years of preparation and, with the help of Clane Fertility Clinic, I got pregnant on my first IVF cycle. I am now well into my second trimester and, so far, all is well, apart from the usual fatigue, nausea, bloating, frequent trips to the loo, mood swings, flatulence, incessant hunger … the list is endless! But who cares; there's a baby growing inside me as I am writing this!

To add to my bliss, my long-time-estranged parents received the news of the impending arrival of their only grandchild with … joy! My mother's exact words were, 'Never mind who was involved or how it happened; the important thing is there's a new baby on the way!' Those words marked the beginning of the inter-generational healing that I never thought was possible. It feels like my family have been given a second chance to rebuild bridges and move on, just like I did. It's true what Henry David Thoreau, the American author, poet, philosopher and abolitionist, once said: 'Every child begins the world again.'

Dil Wickremasinghe

It Takes a Village

After a very tragic death within my family circle almost three years ago, I decided that I was going to come out. After 25 years of marriage, several separations and reconciliations, I knew this was the only way forward.

I have two children, a darling boy, Michael (well, he is a man now), twenty-four, and the most gorgeous daughter, Martha, twelve. These two people are the most important people in my life. I felt it necessary to tell my son first before I told anyone else. I told him, and he took it very well. His best friend, Niamh, was gay, and he had had many long discussions with her about her lifestyle and the difficulties she faced. When I came out to him, he was so supportive and actually sympathised with me as a result of those long discussions he had had with Niamh, some of which had taken place in my own kitchen over hot cups of tea.

Sadly, Niamh took her own life early one Sunday morning in September, months before I came out to my son. It was her death that spurred me on in some ways to let the truth out. You see, she died knowing my secret. Niamh was openly gay and made no qualms about it. One evening after a few glasses of wine (Dutch courage) I told her that I admired her and her bravery to be openly gay. I told her I wished I could be more honest with myself and everyone around me. She asked what I was talking about, so I told her that I had been gay for years, knew it and, at times, lived a covert gay life (during the times I was separated from my then husband).

We had the usual discussions about when I knew, when she knew, her difficulty in telling her family and my difficulty in telling my son. She tried to reassure me that it would be OK, that Michael would understand and that he would love me just the same. I never really believed her. She spoke highly of my son and the love that they had for each other. She talked about how he supported her in her lifestyle, her decisions and even on occasion in her love life. She told me that if anyone would understand my situation it would be him.

We laughed and we cried that night, and I remember hugging her tightly and whispering in her ear that I loved her and asking her to keep my secret. She promised she would and said that it was my decision to keep it in or let it out and no one else's. She promised never to say a word, and she never did.

Once the dust had settled on me coming out to Michael, I asked him if Niamh had ever told him about our conversation that night in the kitchen, but he said she hadn't. In fact, he was very surprised that she had not told him, but he understood all the same. I told him how I wished I could have her back even for just five minutes to tell her how she had paved an easier road for me and to hug her. Just five minutes. RIP Niamh.

When I felt that my son had got his head round the news and that he was comfortable enough with it, I told my parents and my husband of over 25 years. My mother commented to the effect that I had 'never really been happy', while my father said, 'Well, it's not like you're telling us you have cancer or anything.' My father had asked me many years before whether I had 'a problem with men', which of course I had denied.

My husband did not take it well. He was angry that Michael had known for months, that I had known for years but had said nothing, and that I had probably wasted the best part of his life lying to him and trying to 'fix' myself. He sprinted for the door and moved out six weeks later. He did say, though, that he had suspected it for years.

I decided that I was not going to tell Martha, who was then just nine years old, about my sexuality. I felt that it was not necessary. We live in a small town, and she attended an even smaller school. I was worried that if people knew about me, she might receive unwanted attention, in whatever forms that may have taken. I asked everyone involved to shield her from knowing until she was approaching secondary school, whence I determined I would have 'the talk' with her. My family honoured this agreement.

About a year later, I slowly began to introduce my daughter to all things gay. I had discussed with several close friends how to make it easier for Martha to understand when I eventually did tell her. It was my very close friend Louise who suggested that it might help to bring Martha along to some events involving my Running Amach friends. She reminded me on many occasions not to be ashamed of who I am and to not let Martha see me feeling ashamed. We discussed how it was important for her to understand what being gay meant and to allow the rest to fall into place.

From there, Martha and I began the journey. We would sit down together and watch *Modern Family*, an American sitcom. One night I asked her about two of the male characters who are gay and married. 'Martha, what is that all about? Those two men, are they married?'

'Oh yes, they love each other,' she said with a smile. I looked at her, quite puzzled, and asked, 'What about two women? Can they be in love and get married?'

Her reply took a few seconds. I could see her processing her answer in her head. 'Well, um, I don't know. Well, I guess so. Yes, sure of course they can.'

There was no more talk about it, and I let the question and answer linger between us. I was secretly happy that she had come to this conclusion by herself.

We attended GLORIA (an LGBTQ choir) at Christmas in St Patrick's Cathedral, Dublin. Martha was in awe of the whole production. Next, I took her to the International Dublin Gay Theatre Festival to see *The Happy Prince*, a play, I explained, written for children by a very famous playwright called Oscar Wilde, who was gay. I took her to some Running Amach events and walks that were family orientated and told her that the women there would be gay and may or may not have children. I introduced her to several of my gay friends, and when she asked if they were gay, I told her they were. I also brought her to the Eilish O'Carroll *Live Love Laugh* show with my Running Amach friends. Again she welcomed this experience with open arms.

One evening, we arrived home after having been out for a walk with the Running Amach group. I was lighting the fire and asked, 'Well, Martha, what did you think of all the women today?' I was aware that she knew they were gay. Her answer almost made me cry.

'Well,' she said, 'they are all just crazy and loveable, like you.' I decided not to follow up on her statement; I was just happy knowing that she had been made to feel comfortable and welcomed by a wonderful group of 'crazy loveable' women (thanks, girls!).

Another night, as we were sitting in the airport in Madrid waiting to fly home from a holiday, she asked me, 'Why do you like rainbows so much? Aren't they for gay people?'

I responded with a question: 'Why do you think I like rainbows, Martha?'

'Because maybe you're gay …' she said, looking worried.

I asked her if she would be shocked if I was gay, and her response floored me.

'Well, yes; I would be.'

'But would you really be shocked, Martha?'

'Well, no. Oh, I don't know. Why, are you?' she asked, with a quiver in her voice.

'Well, to be truthful, Martha, I am definitely thinking about it. I am trying to figure that out.' I knew she was not ready for my answer, so I just planted another seed. I left that whole conversation in Madrid airport.

Four months after that incident (and almost two years since I had come out to the rest of my family), I was standing in the kitchen, cooking dinner. Martha was sitting at the dining-room table. She turned to me and said, 'Mom, are you ever going to tell me that you're a lesbian?'

I went weak at the knees and took an enormous inhale before answering. 'Well, do you want me to tell you that I am a lesbian?'
'No.'
'Why?' I asked.
'Because I already know,' she said, very matter-of-factly.
'Is that OK?' I asked, with fear in my voice.
'Yeah, you're still my mom, and just because you're gay doesn't make any difference.' I then asked her how long she had known, and her reply was, 'Well, about a year I think.' I felt so relieved! We spoke for a few more minutes about it, but I can't honestly remember what more was said. I just remember feeling terribly proud of her. Then I felt proud of me and the Running Amach women. We had all played a part in my journey to help Martha understand who I am. So I guess I will never have to have that talk with her.

There is an African proverb that says: 'It may take two people to make a child, but it takes a village to raise it.' I'd like to thank my 'village', especially Michael, Louise and Fergal, my friends gay or straight, and my Running Amach women for helping me to raise my child without fear or prejudice and to once again pave my road so that it was and is easier to walk on.

Susan O'Neill

'Je Pense à Toi'

It was Sunday evening, last August bank holiday. I was walking over to the Front Lounge bar in Dublin with my good friend Marie, supporting a fairly nauseating hangover. I don't usually suffer from hangovers, but I blame the pint of Guinness I had at stupid o'clock the previous morning, that on top of every other concoction I had already had. Of course, I've since managed to forgive the Guinness!

Upon our arrival, I was feeling really crappy. I said to my friend, 'You know I need to meet an angel tonight; I'm really not wearing this hangover well.'

Over the course of the evening, we chatted a little, and I sipped on tonic waters in the hope that I'd feel revived sooner rather than later. It was quiet in the place that evening, and I contemplated leaving a few times, saying to my friend, 'Ah, I'd be better off in bed.' A few of my friend's acquaintances came over to our table and started chatting with her, but I was keeping pretty quiet.

I had noticed two girls come and sit at the table next to us. They were talking away and giggling, sipping on pints of Guinness. Every now and then they would look over. It was a nice distraction, I must say. They were beautiful and had a good energy about them. I, being shy, averted my gaze when one of the girls was trying to catch my eye. They kept me amused for a while, and I was intrigued by them. As the night progressed, I noticed definite looks of interest coming in my direction. I didn't really know how to take it. The girl was stunning, and my hangover was lifting.

Eventually, both girls came over to talk to me. One of the girls, from Boston, introduced herself briefly, before introducing her friend from Mexico, Monica. 'She thinks you are sexy, and she wants to know if you have a girlfriend and whether you can speak Spanish,' she said.

I was almost lost for words. All I could manage to say back was, 'No, and no.' I was a bit reluctant to entertain them because I was in a shy and embarrassed state, but I was also a bit blown away. Monica's Boston friend soon left to go to The Dragon, so Monica and I were alone.

She was very sweet and shy herself, with an amazing smile. Her English wasn't great, but we managed to get along with what we had: her broken English and my hopeless school French, which she also speaks. Eventually, it was getting near to closing-up time. We had been chatting for about half an hour. I was heading off with my friend because we were staying in the same accommodation. I tried to tell Monica I had to go, but she wanted me to stay with her. I didn't want to leave her, but I had to.

We shared a kiss outside The Front Lounge, and I searched for a pen in my bag to write my number down, but I couldn't find one. Then, 'Eureka!' Lipstick – the romantic pen! I quickly scribbled down my number, but my friend had already flagged a taxi and was about to head off.

'I gotta go!' I said.

We kissed again and said goodbye.

The next morning, before I headed out of town and back home, I received a text while queueing upstairs in Brown Thomas to buy coffee. The message read: 'Je pense à toi.'

I texted her back: 'Oh wow! I was just thinking of you!'

We exchanged a couple more texts over the course of that week and planned a date for the following Saturday. To make a long story short, we have established a great relationship and have been enjoying the best of times since.

Meeting Monica really proved to me that you just don't know when someone will walk into your life and change it for the better. I think it often happens at the least expected time. Then again, maybe my guardian angel heard my call after all.

Emma

Late Bloomer

I was a 'late-blooming flower', due to a medical trauma in my early childhood. The incident affected me deeply and overshadowed everything else in my life. I was very distracted by the traumatic experience, and recovering from it physically and emotionally was overwhelming. It prevented me from dealing with my feelings about my sexuality for decades.

When I was young, I had never met a gay person. Anyone who spoke of gay people spoke disparagingly about them. Clearly, being gay was not popular or accepted in society. The messages from my community and wider society were negative, and gay people were to be made fun of. Being gay was shrouded in fear, taboo, mystery, revulsion and repulsion. I had a total lack of awareness, exposure and education about gay people and their lifestyles.

Looking back now, I realise I was attracted to other women, but I systematically buried those feelings and refused to acknowledge them. They were nice feelings, but I never talked about them. They were to be afraid of, ashamed of and embarrassed by. I used to think, 'God help me, if anyone found out!'

I dated and dabbled in sexual activity and relationships with men. I was doing what I was expected to do. What I had been socialised to do. I complied with those expectations. But I always held back a large part of my true self. I never gave my whole self to anyone, ever!

When I entered the working world, I began to meet gay people. I worked in the caring profession, and being different

85

was acceptable in my work environment. I remember very clearly having dinner with work colleagues one evening. Someone pointed out a woman and disclosed that she was a lesbian. She was attractive (OK, hot!), and I envied her confidence. I became friendly with other gay colleagues and learned that they were just ordinary decent people like me. They weren't monsters, circus freaks, rejects or outcasts, as I had been led to believe, as I had led myself to believe.

I became friends with gay people, and slowly but surely my unconscious feelings started to surface. It didn't mean I acted on them. In fact, I ignored them most of the time and just got on with my busy life. Then I began meeting gay women through the sports world. Some were out, but most were still in hiding. There was such secrecy around the whole gay issue, which made it near impossible to figure out what a gay lifestyle was like. From time to time, I even went to gay bars with my friends. I was the 'straight' girl my gay friends brought to the gay bars. I was learning, from a very safe position, that the gay world was a lot of fun and included ordinary and extraordinary decent women, just like *moi*. I was slowly becoming more aware of the possibility of accepting that I might be gay.

Following a period of stressful events in my life and at work, I decided to go for counselling. Throughout those sessions, the stressful events I was facing fell into the background and the topic of my sexuality came to the foreground. In particular, I had met a woman who made my stomach flutter. I was too afraid to tell anyone, too afraid to tell her, and too afraid to come out to myself. I spoke to my counsellor about it, who encouraged me to go out 'on the scene' and experiment. No way in hell was I going out on the scene on my own! To experiment? I would be eaten alive, or so I thought. I just did not have the confidence to do it.

I resisted my feelings, out of utter fear. I felt paralysed and stuck. I found the process of coming out to myself very challenging, terrifying, frightening, confusing, despairing, lonely and oh so painful. One day, as I left a counselling session, I passed my local Catholic church. I looked at the church in despair and said silently to God, 'I don't want to be gay.' I could not see how I was going to come out and live a happy life. It was hopeless! I felt such shame. I was suicidal. I didn't want to live my life if it meant being gay.

I have never felt so depressed, isolated, excluded, lonely, afraid and unhappy as I did then. I was despondent that I didn't possess the courage to deal with my feelings or to come out to others. I didn't want to be the 'gay one' in my family or community. It all felt so overwhelming. I was angry with God for making me gay. 'Why, of all things, do I have to be gay? Have I not had enough to deal with in my life?'

I continued going to work, meeting friends, playing sports, travelling and visiting my family. But I was unhappy. I was never going to be blissfully happy in my life; there was the 'little matter' of my strong attraction to a woman. But they were nice feelings, and I couldn't ignore them forever. I wanted to have more of those feelings. It was clear that I needed support and I needed to talk about what I was going through, but I didn't have the guts to admit it to anyone else. I was at cracking point.

Eventually, I told my older sister, who was very supportive and encouraging. She was also accepting of and empathetic to my struggles and fears. She was also not surprised! Then I told another sister. She thought it was 'cool' and exciting. What relief! Gradually, I began to open up a bit more. I started to tell a few friends. Everyone was positive and supportive. Thank God I had picked loving and caring friends.

Following months of slowly coming out to a very select few people, I realised I was fortunate to have positive reactions and support from all of them. That doesn't diminish how hard it was to open up to people about being gay, however; it was cringing at times. Often I would meet up with a friend and 'chicken out' from telling them I was gay. I didn't have the courage to come out to them, even though I had planned to. I would return home feeling more disappointed in myself. Such anguish ... urhhhh!

A year after coming out to my sisters, I decided it was time to come out to my mother. Our relationship was challenging at times, but it was important to me that my mother knew the real and true me. I didn't care if she accepted it or not. I was taking a huge risk of being rejected forever. We were at the cottage one weekend with other family members, and finally we were alone. I told her that I needed to tell her something. She calmly asked, 'What?' and I told her I was gay.

'You're still my daughter, and I still love you,' she responded.

Perfect! We discussed some of the issues I was facing, and she suggested counselling. I told her I had already been. I think inside she was shocked and afraid. I know in my heart that she did not sleep a wink that night. But I felt relieved and unburdened. Later on, my sister told me she had called Mom at the cottage for a chat. My mother told her I had come out to her, and my sister said, 'Yes, I know she was going up to you.'

'No,' my mother said. 'She CAME OUT to me!' My sister finally got it. She was able to support my mother through what I'm sure was devastating news. My gayness was now out, but it was never talked about or mentioned.

What is it like to be in love with a woman? Putting it into words just can't do it justice, so let me use a few metaphors. It's a rainbow of fireworks. It's the Northern Lights. It's experiencing all four seasons at once. It's a spice jar. It's a flash of lightning. It's electricity crackling through your body. It's a physical and emotional symphony. It's explosive, sensual, passionate, nourishing, reviving, a completeness, a yearning fulfilled, a personal wholeness. It's similar to anyone else being in love!

Over the years, I brought my partners home from time to time, and we were always treated with the utmost respect and kindness by all members of my family. We were accepted, and our relationship was accepted, but the word 'gay' was never spoken. My mother never asked about my relationships or spoke about me being gay again.

Many years after I came out, my mother was visiting me. I drove her to visit her friend who was unwell. While I drove, she told me the following story. A few months previously, she had dropped off tickets for a political fundraising event to two very close family friends. She dropped the tickets to their home. A few days later, she arrived home and found the tickets returned with some money in her letter box. She telephoned her friends to ask why they couldn't attend and to thank them for their donation. They told her they couldn't attend because the personal assistant of the politician for whom the fundraiser was being organised was gay, and they could not support 'something like that'. She told me she could not believe their attitude 'in this day and age'. She got into her car, drove to their home and put the money back in their letter box. I was stunned. I was moved. I was delighted! Even today, I have tears rolling down my cheeks while I write this. My mother's behaviour that day told me more than any of the few words she had ever spoken to me about my being gay. It told me that she accepted me, supported me, protected me and prized me. Finally, I exhaled.

Maureen Looney

My Epiphany

Yes, I am one. One of them. One of yours. One who didn't know who she was. Until she came really close, brushed her lips against mine and slowly turned the heat on. I don't know what happened, but two hours later we were still at it, kissing nonstop.

Getting warm, damp, steamy, sticky, sweaty, and feeling, frankly, quite hot! Touching, caressing, discovering and sizzling. Fighting to stay within the safe comfort and limits of our own bloody clothes, because we were in public and giving people a jolly good show!

Me, who had warned her beforehand that I didn't like kissing, that I never even kissed men. Not on the lips, the cheeks or anywhere else. That in maybe fifteen to twenty years I hadn't kissed another soul, because of all that gross saliva exchange going on.

Me, who had spent tons of money on therapy sessions to be told that not liking to be kissed wasn't really that unusual. That some people didn't like kissing, and others didn't like to swear. 'Pretty normal,' said the therapist. 'Let's move to other business and stop worrying about why you don't like kissing. It doesn't mean you are faulty or gay. Maybe a bit rare.'

What does one do with a therapist who doesn't realise one is simply not straight instead of rare? I wish I had had my epiphany before because, by now, I would be richer and also more aware. Instead, I discovered that I quite love kissing. Just not by men.

Her lips were patient, warm, soft, curious, sensual and bare. Never aggressive, overbearing or hasty. Never in a race to get somewhere. We spent over two hours kissing, just on the lips. She never left them to discover new land or new skin to bare. It was magnificent and exquisite. A feast for my insides and my senses. It was the first time I realised what I had been missing. If only I had asked the right sex to kiss me all those years before in a teenage game of truth or dare!

Shades of Gay

Stick Out Your Tongue!

'Stick out your tongue,' she warned. 'If I find a black mark, I will know that you are lying.'

I was five years old, and the contents of the china cabinet lay on the floor, crashed into a thousand pieces. We were five siblings, all lined up, each with an 'I'm-the-innocent-one' look etched onto our tear-stained faces. My mother grabbed the wooden spoon and called each of us in turn to be examined. One by one we shuffled up as if we were bound by an invisible chain. I remember the palpable fear of having a black mark on my tongue. I had nothing to hide, but I still feared that the mark might magically appear, and I would get the blame.

My small brain throbbed as I sought to avoid such a calamity. I resorted to the best defence I could think of – I blabbed. I ratted out my siblings to save myself from the indignity of being branded a liar.

This became my identity: I was the truthful one. What you saw is what you got. I was as straight as a die, no sides; I was just me. I prided myself on my honesty, even though it is only with age that I have been able to wield it as a tool rather than a weapon. I flinch at the thought of my youthful need to be open with people and how I often revealed too much, and to the wrong people. I wore my 'self' on my sleeve, as a badge of honour.

So it is with absolute horror that I now find myself living each day with the heavy burden of a lie. Just one lie, but it is sufficient to make my whole world spin on its axis and change my way of being, thinking and feeling. I am nearing 40, married with several children and living in rural Ireland. None of this is untrue. But, when I add that I am a closet lesbian, then my life feels like one big lie, then those whom I hold dear become victims of my deceit. That is difficult, but the fact that I somehow lied to myself for so long is just galling.

So, how the hell did I get here? Truth be told, I always felt a little different. As a child I was a tomboy and rebelled against all things pink and girlie. It wasn't that I didn't like those things, it was more the fact that they were forced upon me as though they naturally belonged to me, like a tail on a dog or a wing on a bird. If you were a girl you were expected to be this. I didn't like 'this'.

Somehow the early failure of coming up short in my family's expectations made me eager to please. I would have done anything to garner their approval, and this trait still lingers with me today. I decided then that I would be and do everything right. I followed every rule, code and moral teaching. I was the innocent girl, teetotal and virtuous, the virginal bride, the devoted Catholic.

I remember liking boys and girls in pretty much equal measure. I was drawn to women in film and TV but didn't think much of it. I definitely fancied males and made good progress in my pursuit! I was eighteen when I first realised that my feelings for women were more than just liking their character in a programme or liking the clothes they were wearing. I really liked *them*. I thought about going up to Dublin and doing something about it. I had heard of a pub called 'The George' and that was the extent of my knowledge of where I could turn to. It seems laughable today with all the supports that are out there for young people, but that was simply the way it was when I was young.

I still remember when being homosexual could land you in jail, when if you were 'that way inclined' you were a deviant. And while I still had a choice, I decided that that was definitely not the life I wanted. So I chose the other. I believe that my sexuality is and was fluid. I know that in my twenties I was bisexual. To be academic about it, I guess I was 60 per cent attracted to men and 40 per cent to women. I was with my husband and loved him, so it was natural and easier to concentrate on that attraction and ignore the other.

Except, it wouldn't stay ignored. Before having my first child, I rapidly began to feel that I needed to look at what I wanted out of life. I allowed myself to contemplate another way of being and planned to reach out and talk to someone, but I bottled it.

Shortly after I became pregnant, and for the next ten years, I was consumed by my maternal and wifely duties. During this time I largely 'forgot' about my dilemma. That does not mean that I think a person's sexuality is trivial, but when you lose yourself, it's pretty darn easy to lose your sexual identity too.

In the past few years I have changed career paths and, in doing so, I had to do a lot of training requiring self-reflection. This awakened in me a sense of who I am and how I missed being me. In the midst of all this self-examination I was hit with the realisation that on the spectrum of sexuality I had moved way beyond the point I was at before. I now felt that my attraction to women was predominant and almost completely pervasive. Thankfully, I am still capable of intimacy with my husband, but it is increasingly difficult. I struggle with what I am. I mean, what am I? I don't feel comfortable saying I am heterosexual because I am definitely not. I think 'lesbian' sounds odd, since I have never so much as rubbed noses with a woman, but 'bisexual' seems disingenuous too. I really feel that I am more gay than straight, yet I don't fit into either world. I am neither an arse nor an elbow!

I find that I am going about my daily routine feeling a fraud. I am keeping a massive secret, and I can't see how I can tell the ones I love. I am caught in a vicious cycle. I told my husband about my attractions very early on in our relationship. His first reaction was delight; he saw it as a sexual aid for us. When I told him that I felt it wasn't just a fantasy, he promptly reminded me that I was married and, so, I should forget about it. 'You can't do anything about it anyway so just ignore it.' Thus, while he knows how I feel, he reckons it's a conversation that has been dealt with, and I can't bring it up again. This has left me to figure it out on my own in secret, which has put a vast distance between us.

My attempts to reach out for help have been mixed. Is there something about lesbian women that makes them slow to return emails? The first place I rang was Gay Switchboard Ireland, but it was answered by a man who was of the view that you were either gay or not and I would have done something about it by now if I was. To say I was crushed and more than a little embarrassed doesn't quite cut it. Thankfully, I rang again the following week and got a lovely lady who gave me some ideas, including joining Running Amach.

My second contact was with a woman who took three weeks to get back to my email and then accidently cc'd my email to another group working in this area. I was mortified and pretty paranoid that my private details were out. Luckily, she managed to get them to delete my email, and I continued my 'research'.

In the early days, I looked to the internet to help me understand my situation. I was shocked at how many sites were vitriolic against people who identify as bisexual, and saw the term 'sexual tourist' quite a lot. While I was contemplating coming out, I began to wonder whether I really had somewhere to come 'in' to once I made my move. Would I be accepted?

Initially, I was all over the place. I even googled 'how to know if you are lesbian'. Yeah, I know – cringe, cringe! I learned about the plethora of really good support groups in Dublin, Cork and Galway, but nothing that was close to me. You can't just say to your husband that you are going to Dublin (which is two hours away) for a meeting at 7.30 p.m. without a pretty good excuse. So going to the Outhouse or any of the Running Amach meetings in Dublin was just not an option for me. I felt isolated and stuck. I trawled the internet and found the excellent Gaelick site, which allowed me to engage as me. When I mentioned my predicament, I got a lot of support, which really helped.

Recently I went to a counsellor who immediately suggested that perhaps I just admired women and didn't really fancy them. She then suggested that I was using this 'notion' to avoid dealing with my real problems of stress and exhaustion. Christ, if I didn't have this hanging over me I wouldn't be stressed and exhausted! She recounted an example that women sometimes respond to traumatic experiences by turning to lesbianism. Since I haven't experienced any trauma, I am none the wiser!

Consequently, I have had to reassess everything I thought I knew about myself. I used to congratulate myself on the fact that I had never ever looked at another man in the past twenty years. I began to realise that this wasn't due to my devotion to my husband; it was simply because I don't fancy any other men. That said, I have never really allowed myself to look at women in that way either. I always closed down any such thoughts almost as soon as they entered my head. One of the biggest changes I've noted since allowing my mind to wander is how often it wanders now. Being nearly 40 and being a 'virgin' is not an easy place to be.

You may wonder what my intentions are. Then you can join the queue. The more I allow myself to feel the feelings I have, the more isolated I am becoming. I ask myself why I am reaching out to other lesbians. Am I hoping to get lucky? But, then, seriously, what self-respecting lesbian is going to engage with a middle-aged, married, closeted, virgin, wannabe lesbian with kids? How would I start a conversation? 'My husband doesn't understand me'? Please!

Having said that, I would be lying if I claimed that I don't spend a lot of time thinking about what it would be like to be in a relationship with another woman. I am saddened when I think that I will probably never know what that is like. Leaving my husband is one thing, but my home and children? Being attracted to women doesn't justify that. The simplest solution would be if I could come to some sort of peace with my attractions and put them back into the box that I found them in. However, I genuinely feel liberated at last for having acknowledged my feelings, and I'm fearful that I might lose myself again and regret the missed opportunity to experience clarity, freedom, identity, pride, sensuality, relationship, understanding, friendship … and love?

So I will continue to muddle through and get support where I can get it. Writing this is a kind of therapy to help me along. I find it amusing and sad that in the unlikely event of this ever being printed I shan't be displaying my work proudly for my loved ones to see. It will be hidden with all those other thoughts and feelings that I cannot share but wish I could. Sometimes I wish I did have a black mark on my tongue. It would be a relief to tell the truth again.

Nuala

Storm in a China Cup

How excited was I? It was the spring of 2008, and I was off to tour China. Visits to the Great Wall, the Terracotta Army, Shanghai, Beijing and the Yangtze River, as well as a trip through the Three Gorges awaited me. It was a trip I'd longed for and waited to do for some years. At long last it was booked and paid for. I was going with one of my closest pals, Claire. When I say we were great pals, we truly were very close indeed. We had known each other for over seven years and had been on holidays several times a year together, even with each other's parents. Claire was so close to my parents they called her their adopted daughter and said that they had included her in their wills.

So there we were, two great pals with our next great adventure planned, and getting more excited as the day of departure grew ever closer.

Six weeks previously, I had split up from a long-term relationship, one that was probably longer than it should have been. Shortly after, I was out one evening, not feeling particularly sociable, when a girl walked across the room and started to chat with me. I wasn't in as friendly a mood as I would normally be, so I only reluctantly engaged in conversation. As the chat continued, I started to thaw a little and ease into the flow of the conversation. Despite myself, I started to enjoy the company of my new-found comrade, Judy. Even though bed had beckoned at 11 p.m., I found that all of a sudden it was 4.30 a.m. and definitely time to retire. After exchanging phone numbers, I bid Judy goodnight and went on my way.

The following weeks consisted of daily calls with Judy, which culminated in a dinner date. I felt myself falling quickly and deeply in love with her. The feeling was very much mutual and something that I never thought would happen to me. I'd never been in love before. I even started to think about what future possibilities there were for us. I was filled with tingly excitement at the prospect, and not the heretofore panic and desire to run in the opposite direction.

So there I was on a plane on the much-awaited trip to China. Claire and I were full of excited chatter. The first few days of our trip were full of awe and wonder at the incredible things we were seeing and experiencing. Judy would enter my thoughts daily and stay in them from dawn to dusk. I had never revealed to a soul my feelings towards women. All throughout my twenties I had dated men and gone out with men, and this had been very much a part of my very 'straight' life. There were no lesbians in my social circle, so it was a completely alien concept to my family and wide circle of friends.

Given that I was rapidly approaching my forties, combined with the intensity of the feelings I was having for Judy, I thought I needed to share it with someone. There I was on holiday with Claire, who, although straight, had herself at one point shared a house with a lesbian. So who better to be the first person to open up my soul to and to reveal my deepest, darkest secret to? On an internal flight, I opened up to my closest friend. I revealed to her that I had met a girl whom I was now dating and had very strong feelings for. A few questions followed: What's her name? How did you meet? Does anyone else know? Followed by 'It doesn't make any difference to me', and 'I suspected you might be gay. I'm happy I was right!' It was really more about Claire and how smug she was for guessing at my sexuality than any real compassion as to how I might be feeling. However, I did have a sense of relief, as I had now told someone my big, dark secret and things seemed to be OK.

Who could have predicted what would ensue over the following days? We were sharing a twin bedroom, and suddenly I noticed that Claire would take her clothes into the bathroom to change and re-emerge fully dressed, as if she feared that I would be eyeing her up. I couldn't believe it. How naive! Then one evening before dinner Claire announced, 'Ya know; this will be our last holiday together. When people find out that you're gay, they might think I'm gay too, so we won't ever be going on holiday together again.'

I couldn't believe my ears. What happened to 'it doesn't make any difference to me; I knew anyway'? My jaw dropped and I gasped, 'Are you serious? Surely you can't be serious! Oh my God, that is the most homophobic thing I have ever heard.'

This was greeted with a further shocking response: 'How dare you call me a homophobe. Fuck you! I shared a house with a lesbian, so I'm definitely not a homophobe.'

'Whoopie doo for you! You can tick that box forever. Oooh, I lived with a lesbian so I'm not homophobic!'

I know my response wasn't the most mature in the world, but how dare she? I'd never been so insulted, disappointed and saddened in my whole life. The next couple of days were dark days for me, filled with a deadly silence and much changing of clothes in the bathroom. I felt lost and alone. Mostly, I just cried myself to sleep at night.

On the third day after this horrible exchange of words, I was making my way down to dinner. I left the room before Claire and took the lift to the ground floor to make my way to the restaurant. As the elevator door opened, the tour guide was on the other side and said, 'Oh, can you tell Claire I've sorted that change of flight for her and she needs to be ready to leave at 6 a.m.?'

'Pardon?' I replied.

'Claire's leaving in the morning and the flight has now been confirmed.'

I managed to squeak out an 'OK, I'll tell her' and quickly continued on my way to join our four fellow travellers at the dinner table.

Claire appeared a few minutes later. I couldn't hold it in any longer. Tears had started to trickle down my cheeks. Our travelling colleagues looked at me in wonder and someone asked, 'Are you OK? What's happened?'

Through the tears I heard myself say, 'I've just told Claire I'm gay, so she's flying home in the morning.' My voice trailed away. Michael, an older member of the group with bad hearing, was sitting at the other end of the table. He asked, a little startled, 'What did she just say?' His question was greeted with no verbal response, but he received a swift kick under the table from his wife, who shot him a look that could only be interpreted as 'Shut the fuck up!' I was crying hard at this point. I left the table, and moments later Claire left in another direction.

I called Judy in floods of tears to describe, through my sobbing, my experiences over the past few days, which were far from the China experience I had dreamed of and hoped for. There and then I decided that when I got home I was going to tell my parents and family that I'm gay. They are the people who matter the most in the world to me. I had hit rock bottom, and there was no longer any risk in revealing the true me. As I thought about returning to Judy, I imagined our lives together and wanted to share our feelings with the people who matter the most.

Lisa Dwyer

Thank God for Marian Finucane!

It wasn't until my brother's wedding in Tipperary last summer that I was reminded, to my great amusement during his wedding speech, of the confusion surrounding his coming out to our father ten years previously, during which I was accidentally outed as well. You see, unlike my brother, who felt the time was right for him to tell our father, I felt absolutely no urgency to come out to him, having already confided in my close friends and most of my siblings.

As later recounted to me by my brother, his weekend trip to Tipperary started off as per usual with dinner at home followed by a visit to the local pub. However, it wasn't until the early hours of Sunday morning that the conversation between father and son really started to flow. Our father had apparently noticed a change in my brother and sensed that something was up. Arriving into the kitchen on Saturday night after the customary few pints in the local, our father headed straight for the kitchen press, produced a bottle of Paddy's and announced, 'Right, there's something wrong with you, so we'll not go to bed until that bottle's empty.'

My brother apparently didn't need much persuading and sat down sheepishly while our father poured the first two glasses of whiskey, which they both drank silently. He then poured another round, which my brother started to gulp down nervously. Eventually, he started to mumble that, yes, he had something to tell him.

Our father then appeared to have a eureka moment and interrupted him, saying, 'Did you get a girl in trouble? Is that it?'

My brother mumbled, 'No, that's not it.' Realising it was now or never, he said, 'I've been going out with someone for a good while now, and it's not a girl; it's a fella.'

There was a long period of silence during which more whiskey was consumed. After a time our father asked, 'What's his name?'

'James.'

'Jimmy … right. Where's he from?' Our father permanently christened James 'Jimmy' from that evening onwards.

'Donegal.'

My brother thought he detected a slight sigh of relief at that. Country people, after all, tend to have a more favourable disposition towards other country folk!

Over the next while, my brother started to explain how he had met 'Jimmy', when they started going out, and how they had moved in together. Our father continued to nod his head silently, listening intently and asking the odd question. More whiskey was poured while my brother talked and our father listened. Then slowly our father started telling stories about his own father, a very difficult man by all accounts, and how they had never talked. Our father always swore he would never be that type of father to his own children.

Eventually, the talking stopped and there was silence.

After a minute or so, our father looked up from the table as if something important had suddenly dawned on him.

'You know, you can't help having that auld thing … you can be born with that. Didn't Marian Finucane do a programme on it the other day? And you hear of parents turning their backs on their own children because of it. God, isn't that terrible?'

My brother smiled with relief as he watched our father, a 70-year-old farmer from Tipperary, slowly try to get his head around his son's announcement, thanking God for Marian Finucane and Paddy's whiskey at the same time. They continued to chat for another hour or so and eventually finished their drinks and went to bed.

Next morning, our other brother, John, was up and about the farm. He came in and was sat having his breakfast in the kitchen when our father joined him. They ate breakfast silently, sipping their mugs of tea. Eventually, our father looked up at John and announced, 'So, have you heard the news?'

To which John gruffly responded, 'No, what news?'

'Brian's after telling me he's with a fella.'

Our brother looked at our father, confused for a moment, then sighed impatiently and slowly shook his head. 'No … no … no. You have it all mixed up. Brian's not with a fella. He's not gay. It's Liz that's gay!'

You see, I had already been home a few weeks previously and had come out to my brother John and his girlfriend, but not to our father.

My father (never one to forget a conversation no matter how much alcohol has been consumed) was adamant, and shook his head.

'No, I'm telling you. Brian sat here in this kitchen drinking whiskey with me last night and told me he's seeing a fella called Jimmy from Donegal.'

This was certainly news to my brother, who wasn't aware of Brian's sexuality at the time.

My father then looked a bit confused and said, 'Liz is gay?'

So my coming out to my father was accidental and by default really. There was no big defining moment or conversation between us. Rather, over the years he has learned to accept me and my brother for who we are and has grown comfortable with this. At one stage, he even speculated whether that 'auld thing' possibly came from our mother's side. Our mother, who had passed away many years previously, unfortunately didn't get to offer her opinion on the matter.

Thinking back over the last ten years, I see instead a series of small moments, a nod of the head, a smile, a comment, a question, where my father, in his own quiet and non-judgemental way, has accepted me for who I am. I realise now that this is one of his most endearing qualities, and not something to be taken for granted.

Every now and then, I like to imagine that moment in a country kitchen in Tipperary on a Sunday morning, as a father and son make a mutual discovery. It makes me think of other country kitchens, mothers, fathers, sons, daughters, brothers, sisters, aunts, uncles, nieces, nephews, husbands and wives.

It makes me smile and gives me hope.

Liz Burns

The Beach

Fran arranged to meet a long-time friend for a walk on the beach and a chat at 12.30 p.m. on Friday. That was the text she sent to Mary, who replied, 'OK'. They had fallen out over five years previously and had not spoken since. Mary had tried to contact Fran many times over the years, even during social gatherings, but Fran would walk away if Mary was in the same room, or she would avoid going to dinner parties if she thought Mary might turn up.

The first time Fran met Mary was on holiday in Nice, at a friend's fortieth birthday party. A group of friends flew off for four days to celebrate and have the craic. She instantly fell for her, thought she was amazing and beautiful, and they became good friends.

Fran found herself staring out her kitchen window, remembering how she felt at that time and the fun they had had on holiday, going over and over it in her mind, when she finally realised Mary was more than just a friend. She remembered on holiday looking at Mary on the beach in her socks. Socks! Who wears socks on a beach, she thought. Mary did. Fran smiled to herself, remembering. While all the girls laughed and chatted away, Fran found herself staring in admiration at Mary and her socks.

Friday came, and Fran was anxiously waiting to meet Mary. She pottered around the house, passing time that seemed to be infinite. 'Why the hell do I feel the need to put myself through this?' she thought to herself. 'Am I bloody mad? Cancel it ... just get over it … cancel it!' she thought to herself. But she didn't cancel.

The time came. Fran got in her car, holding back the tears, knowing what she wanted to tell Mary, but how? She felt physically sick at the prospect of telling her after all this time and imagining the reaction she might receive. The years had gone by, but every day she thought of her friend Mary and wished she was with her. It wasn't to be, however, and she had struggled with it for years.

Fran had been married for over twenty years to Derrick, with whom she had a son. She remembered the angst she had felt about finally telling him, and wondered about how he must have been feeling. He said nothing, just stared at their family photo on the mantelpiece.

Fran strolled along the beach watching each wave that rolled in as she waited, every minute feeling like forever. Waiting for Mary. Mary was late. Thoughts rolled in and out of her mind like the waves. She remembered all the poems Mary had sent her.

'She must have had some feelings for me; why else would she have written them? And why did she write them? Did I imagine the whole thing?' She began to doubt herself. 'I'm going home. Why am I putting myself through this?' she thought. 'Sure, anyway, the last time we met, Mary ran. I mean, ran away! Even when I called her back to see if she was OK, she got upset and walked away again. That was the last time we spoke,' she remembered.

As Fran turned to walk back towards her car, she saw Mary walking down the steps towards her. They awkwardly walked towards each other and greeted one another with a nervous smile. Then they walked along the beach together, chatting about the weather and how lovely the morning was. Fran had not noticed what sort of morning it was till Mary pointed it out. It could have been snowing for all she cared. As Mary chatted away about this and that, Fran got even more anxious to the point where Mary finally stopped and asked her if she was OK.

'I'm fine. Really, I'm grand,' she replied, but she just stood rooted to the spot, as if time stood still. She knew this was the time. Looking straight at Mary she began to explain why she had been avoiding her all this time.

Mary said, 'I knew you were avoiding me, Fran, but I just didn't know why or what I had done.'

Fran stopped her and said, 'Mary, this is really difficult for me, but I feel I need to tell you and explain why I have backed away and not spoken to you all this time.'

Mary stood looking at her friend as she tried to explain.

'In the last few months,' Fran continued, 'I … I have come out … to Derrick and one or two good friends. I'm gay.' A moment passed and Fran continued. 'I wanted to meet up and explain why I have been distant with you. I began to … have feelings for you.' Just then she paused. 'There, I've said it,' she thought.

Mary listened but said nothing, so Fran continued. 'Being married and a mother, I have battled with how I felt, so I had to back away from our friendship. I'm sorry, but that's how I felt.'

Fran really wanted to say that she had fallen in love with Mary, but she couldn't find the words. They walked on in silence for a while. Finally Mary said, 'You're so brave, Fran, but I missed our friendship. Look, Fran, I hope we can be friends again, but I don't feel the same way for you. I'm not gay. I did think maybe this was the reason you didn't want to speak to me.'

Fran thought to herself just at that moment, 'What the hell have I done? You bloody fool!' They walked along the beach together. Fran was relieved she had finally told Mary, but she was heartbroken that Mary didn't love her back.

After a time she said, 'You sent me so many poems.'

'Oh, they were nothing.'

'OK.'

Mary continued chatting away as though nothing had happened. Fran just listened. They walked to the end of the beach, then turned back.

'Maybe we can go for a coffee sometime, Fran?' Mary said.

'Sure. Anyway, good to see you're keeping well, Mary.' They had reached the steps.

'I have a few things in town to do, so I'll head off,' Mary said. They wished each other well and promised to meet up for a coffee sometime. And that was it.

'It's over,' Fran thought.

She watched Mary walk up the steps to her car, feeling both sad and relived. She lit a cigarette and stood watching the waves roll in and out, hoping she could now move on. Finally!

Pauline Byrne

The Bottle Lost at Sea

Now that I'm about to see you again, I get goosebumps just thinking of you sitting quietly alone, reading a book and waiting for me. And I can feel my heart already racing with anticipation, the blood thickening and raising a fever that beats in my throat, affecting my breathing and my ability to speak and be me.

As I sit in front of you, I feel my senses are heightened, and I become overwhelmed by this yearning that tingles my stomach, before slowly filling up every drop of my blood, crawling into every inch of my skin and awakening it. In the meantime, your confidence grows. I can see your body language responding to mine, mellow and submissive yet overpowering me.

Your arms are not only uncrossed but wide open. You are sitting back, relaxed and confident in the chair, one arm on its back and the other arm on the table. You smile and look down at me, in defiance almost, undoubtedly aware of your powers and your unspoken allure. Aware that I am yielding to you, that I crave you and that I want you. That to see you in total control and so comfortable in your own skin is turning me on and stirring waves of heat and currents beneath my clothes, breaking me and making me shiver. Damp, warm and dizzy. Aroused to the point of wishing we were somewhere else, where I could just stretch across those few centimetres to your hand and slightly touch it, almost by accident.

And notice whether my fingers are welcomed or feared. Discover if you are willing to let me get closer. Close enough to feel your breath on my skin. Close enough to touch your lips with my fingers and slowly let them wander down your neck. To the place where I can feel your pulse quickening and your will fading, gently and unrushed. Like a caress unsure of its strength or its power. To touch skin as soft as mine with my lips and chase it beyond the confines of your blouse with the smallest of pressures.

Just enough to see the finest of hairs rising and your body tensing and your eyes closing. Capitulating and leaving you to my mercy. This is all I can see when I sit in front of you. This is why I can't stop looking into your eyes without feeling defeated, captivated and conquered, but also hopeful and worthy.

And now you come forward and lean on the table. You look straight ahead instead of at me. I know that if we lock eyes at this very moment, we will be lost. I try to make a joke to lighten the undeniable chemistry that is weighing on us like an unexpected burden, drawing us closer, circling us and keeping us on the edge. We are unable to look straight at each other because of our inauspicious present and our uncertain future. But you keep staring at the wall behind me because it is safer than anywhere else.

Suddenly, unexpectedly, you say you have to leave, as if you have just come to your senses and realised something is wrong. I can't retain you and I don't even try. I stand up to give you a farewell kiss, only it becomes something else along the way. Maybe it was catching your eyes checking me out after finally accepting that your instincts were right and that I like women too. Maybe it was the butterflies in my stomach that multiplied in their hundreds when I laid eyes on you again, after weeks of slowly cocooning in your absence, waiting for your presence to bring them to life and set them free, rushing through my veins, quickening my heartbeat and weakening my will power.

The farewell kiss on your cheek that was meant to be friendly and innocent, like all my kisses to friends and family, becomes a moment of unexpected awkwardness between us. For the first time ever, my body betrays me, disobeys me and refuses to comply with social norms and pleasantries, as if it knows we are well beyond that, at a point of no return that started when I first laid eyes on you on that Saturday morning outside that pub. You were sitting confidently on the picnic table with your hair all pulled back and your mountain gear on, waiting for us to arrive. I said I liked a woman giving us the course, and you looked up at me and smiled.

We spoke effortlessly after that, until I said I should go with the others and you asked me to stay instead. That's how I knew I was done. We looked at each other, and I sensed my heartbeat quickening and my body awakening and rediscovering a tingling and a yearning that grew stronger as the weekend went on, encouraged by your closeness and by the way you kept looking at me, as if we had already met, or as if we were somehow meant to meet.

I didn't know how much you meant to me until I got back home and tears started rolling down my cheeks at the thought of not seeing you ever again – ridiculous, crazy, absurd, foolish and irrational tears that kept falling uncontrollably, as if I had lost a loved one to a sudden death, as if one of my closest friends was moving continents, as if my body recognised you for who you are to me, even though my mind couldn't explain it or stop my tears or end my mourning, a mourning that continued until I contacted you again. Ignoring you was no longer an option. You had just appeared like a genie out of a bottle and I couldn't put you back in and throw you out to sea. I couldn't wait for you to come back in a few years, after my tears had dried and your memory had faded.

My body is telling me that you matter, maybe more than anybody or anything in my life has mattered, more than the marriage, the heartache, the pain, the gossip, the hurt, all the things that would remain safely locked away with you if I just put you back into that bottle and throw you away, as I have done with all your predecessors.

I never allowed myself to get to know them, not even as acquaintances, because they were too free, too confident, too happy in their own female skin, and I was scared. I was terrified that they would find me out, terrified that they would realise that I belonged to their tribe and come searching for me to try and win me over, as they once or twice did. I couldn't bear that.

The fear of knowing was too high and the bliss of ignorance too keen, so I made do with what I had, a half-filled bottle lost at sea that nobody could see, not even me, and a life of buried treasures, buried feelings.

I worked relentlessly, tirelessly and constantly in attempts to bury my feelings. Over time, I bought lots of chocolates, drank lots of wine and stopped caring what I looked like. I didn't care even when my husband said I was too fat to have sex. But during all this time, the bottle lost at sea kept getting filled with my desires until it sank one day and I couldn't breathe. That's when I became a castaway, that's when therapy kicked in and gave me armbands to go and swim, and oxygen to dive really deep.

That's where I was when we met, trying to find this bottle of mine to bring myself back to me. But over that weekend you found it for me and brought it to the shore. Instead of handing it in, you simply set it free, bringing my body and soul back to life at the age of 42.

Maybe because I started listening to my body more I can't ignore it now. Maybe that is why now, as I am kissing you goodbye, I linger next to you and your skin after the kiss is over, unable to move or react, as if my body knows it belongs here. The unspeakable wisdom of a body that knows what it aches for before the mind has registered it. The moment doesn't last long, but it is long enough to hear your voice tremble as you turn to say goodbye. That's how I know you know. I won't kiss you again until a few weeks later, when the butterflies are back in their thousands. Next time you will kiss me back.

For Emily, who got me here.

Since I met you I have become a better mum, a better listener and a better person. I am happier, calmer, braver and wiser. I have climbed many more mountains and brought my children with me as you once asked me to do, and as your mother did with you. It is because of your words and your words of wisdom that we connected, but it is for laughter and your playful nature that I have stayed.

Angeles

The Gayest Family on the Campsite

I reluctantly went on a family holiday to sunny France at the awkward age of seventeen. Having just sat my final exams at school, I would much rather have been engaging in self-destructive behaviour with like-minded friends at home.

Deep down, I always knew I was attracted to women. It was as natural to me as liking a certain scent or being drawn to a particular song. I never really questioned whether I was bisexual or lesbian, I just felt attracted to people regardless of their gender. This did not sit well with me as an Irish teenager, however. The society with which I was familiar and the religious views which had been forced upon me did not tolerate homosexuality. My parent's expectations of me didn't include my being gay. I feared that the world would not accept me. I did not feel secure or confident enough in my own skin to act out my true identity. It is incredible how one can suppress one's identity, even to oneself. In hindsight, it inevitably causes inner turmoil, if not self-destructive patterns.

At the campsite in the south of France, I was quickly befriended by two Irish girls whose tent was adjacent to ours. The two sisters introduced me to their younger brother, their mother, and their mother's friend. I warmed to these people instantly and felt comfortable in their company. I spent a lot of time with this family over the following two weeks, eating breakfast with them, going on day trips and playing board games in the evening. We laughed a lot and had open, deep conversations and debates about life. There was a bond between them that I knew was rare. They had a certain rapport, patience and warmth, which I think most families strive to achieve. Of course, I knew their lives were not perfect, as one of the daughters told me that they no longer had a relationship with their father. I didn't ask any questions, I just reflected on how sad and angry that must have made them feel.

I was probably one of the last people on the campsite to cop on that my newfound friends' mother was in a relationship with her female 'friend'. Even the day spent at the beach with them, when the mother simply wore Speedos and her butch haircut, I didn't realise what an unconventional family had taken me under their wing. It wasn't until about a week into the holiday that I learned these two beautiful women were in fact a couple. Having strolled into their tent one humid afternoon, I noticed them resting on a double bed. Lying side by side, asleep and intimate, I was greeted with the beautiful image of a lesbian couple taking a siesta on their summer holidays. I didn't ask any questions; I just reflected on what a wonderful family I had had the privilege of meeting.

This encounter opened my eyes and my mind and gave me strength. I saw first-hand how two women can be loving and nurturing parents together. It was magnificently normal. The experience taught me to accept myself as I was, and to allow the feelings and desires that I had to flow. This self-acceptance was a huge step in my development as a young woman. It empowered me and excited me. It encouraged me to explore my sexuality without shame.

I soon came out to my closest friends. I was overwhelmed by their acceptance and surprised by a few female and male friends who confided in me that they too questioned their sexual orientation of being 'straight'. I wanted nothing more than to fall in love, be loved, and to share my life with someone who saw the beauty and honesty in me.

Fifteen years on, I can still remember the giddy feeling that enveloped us on that holiday. I am now the mother of a beautiful young daughter. We live alone and no longer have a relationship with her father. My daughter has me, and I her. The bond between us is tangible. She knows she is loved without boundaries. I know what it feels like to love another human being unconditionally. I know how hard a mother works to create a safe and nurturing home for her child. I would like nothing more than to meet and fall in love with a beautiful woman in the near future, preferably while I am still in my prime! To welcome somebody I admire and trust enough into my little family, someone who deserves my love and the love of my daughter. She would have to be one special lady! I can imagine us, sitting at our dinner table, talking, smiling and growing.

There are times when I do fear for how my daughter will be seen, through the judgemental eyes of others. I worry that narrow-minded parents who refuse to accept the love that can exist between a same-sex couple will pass on their arrogance to their children, empowering them with a bully-like attitude. And, of course, there are those who believe gay couples should not have the right to raise a family. But the fear and anger I feel towards such prejudice does not last long when I recall that summer in France.

And when I do meet a woman, and our love unfolds, I will welcome those who would condemn our life to sit at our table with us and see just how natural and beautiful the love between two women can be. What a blessing it would be for a young girl to have two mothers! Two powerful, nurturing role models, living their lives with honesty and pride.

Julie Field (aka Julie Goo)

The Other Half of Our Oranges

I met Orla at the first dinner ever organised by Running Amach at the start of 2010. I am from France and had been living in Dublin for eight years. She is from Clondalkin and had been living there for 29 years. Orla was nothing like me, but in some ways she was just like me: a lesbian with a lot of straight friends, no interest in the scene, but still with a need to find her peers and socialise with them. The dinner went very well, and we all felt at ease after a few minutes of uneasy looks that seemed to ask, 'Is it weird to be meeting twenty lesbians on the internet?'

Being brutally honest, Orla spent the evening slagging off a 21-year-old for being 21, and also for being from Killiney. 'I'm sure you have like Louis Vuitton bags and shit; go on admit to it.' We opened our eyes wide as the girl replied 'No, no, no ... well, just one!' A great night altogether!

We joined quite a lot of other meetups together. Orla called me 'Frenchie' and made a habit of slagging me for being ... well, everything really, depending on the day of the week, and the hour of the day. We shared a lot of late-night – and, I must say, inebriated – hilarity, and a good few Sunday-morning giggles over Irish breakfasts. I brought her back raclette cheese from France for Christmas. *L'amitié, quoi!* (Friendship, what!)

I had been single for nearly two years, and although I was meeting a lot of women via Running Amach, nobody ever seemed to shake me up. The first time that Brónagh came to a meetup, it was clear that she was the most attractive woman in the room, and she was also completely unaware of it. She was just a bundle of nerves. I looked at her and thought to myself, 'Gosh, she is pretty. And, damn, I don't feel anything! It's been two years now, though. Maybe something's wrong with me. Maybe I'm really not a lesbian after all? Should I go back to guys?'

This was starting to be weird. A few days later, I received a message from Orla that read: 'I have a date on Wednesday. Any hints for conversation topics? What if I say the wrong thing? You know the way my jokes can be sometimes.'

I thought to myself, 'She's so nervous; that's not like her.' I told her that if the date in question got offended by her sense of humour, she should be the one to run away, anyway.

A short while later, Orla announced that she and Brónagh had started going out together. I saw the shy and cute couple a few times and caught a look of enamoured incredulity on Orla's face while she was looking at Brónagh, as if she couldn't quite believe that this was really happening to her. There's nothing like seeing a good friend blush with happiness. Next thing I know (well, six months later), they're having a birthday party that turns into an engagement one, and I'm told to expect a wedding invitation. I love lesbians!

After nearly a decade of life in Dublin, I decided to leave Ireland and move to Barcelona. It was a surprisingly seamless move, considering that I didn't know anybody and didn't quite speak Spanish. I really got to experience that when you are a positive and confident adult – something that my years of ups and downs in Dublin had eventually, and quite miraculously, turned me into – the world just shapes itself around you. I felt like I was on autopilot, and I quietly settled into what felt like just the right place for me.

Incidentally, another group like Running Amach popped up in the Barcelona section of the MeetUp website, a few weeks before I was due to arrive there. On my first week in Barcelona I attended the first meetup of that group. My Spanish was pretty horrendous then, but the first person I met there was Marta, a Catalan girl who had lived in Dublin for eight years. How is that for a world that shapes itself around you? I quickly went on to become the Erin of Barcelona's Running Amach (Erin being the assistant organiser of Running Amach (and no, it isn't called *Corriendo Fuera* – 'Running Out' – it's just called 'Barcelona L Friends') and started to organise different activities with the group.

On our third meeting, Katyna joined us. She is from Mexico and had been living in Barcelona for seven years at the time. We all immediately loved her sense of humour and quickly found ourselves having a great, animated conversation, even though most of us were perfect strangers. We had coffee, went to the cinema, then on for a bite to eat and a drink. The conversation flew from coming-out stories to a debate on homosexual genes. Four of us stayed on, and I was feeling a natural connection similar to what I have with old friends. I was also grateful that all of them could speak English, so there was no barrier.

Then, quite suddenly, as Katyna was talking, I noticed the perfect shape of her lips and couldn't take my eyes off them. It felt like my look had tilted a little, and I thought, 'Hang on a minute; there is something here.' As she was talking, about what I can't remember, her face lit up with cute enthusiasm. I felt a strange fascination for her; it was like I was recognising someone I already knew rather than looking at the face of someone I had just met that same day.

Shortly after, as I was lying on my sofa thinking about this intriguing woman I had met, I thought, 'Why not say it, if this is how you feel?' I sent her a simple message saying that I was glad to have met her, that I had had a great time, and that I hoped she would join other meetups soon. It was pretty non-committal, yet quite daring given my usual standards of passivity.

About four minutes later, she called me.

'Hi. I just got your message and, yes, I feel the same. I will see you soon for sure.'

I think that this reaction well represents Katyna's attitude of simple honesty and a total absence of game-playing when it comes to feelings. We met again at another couple of meetups with the group and slowly got to know each other. One night we went out for drinks with the group, then on to a club. We were all dancing and messing around. Then she came close to me. We started dancing slowly, and the floor disappeared from under our feet, together with the people and the music and everything else around us. I have no idea what time it was or how long it lasted, I just know that for a long time we didn't kiss; we just kept dancing cheek to cheek and smiling at what we both knew then.

I spent the following days in a state of emotional shock. About three days in, I knew that this was it. I knew that I wanted to be with her and enjoy the magnificent ride of life awaiting us. I felt no fear spending all of our first ten days and nights together. For the first time, I put no filter between my heart and the words that came out of me. I was physically sick with the strength of it all. I couldn't eat or sleep much and absolutely could not work.

Facebook message to Orla: 'Orla! Are you online? Well, I just wanted to say that I've met (erm biblically met) a magnificent woman and somehow felt like telling you.'

We exchanged a few messages. I explained how in love I suddenly found myself, how surprising yet how right it felt. I remembered this autopilot feeling I had when coming to Barcelona. Orla said that she felt the universe had tilted just the right way to put her on her way, and that is exactly how I felt. Orla was the first person I wanted to share this with because I knew that this is how she had felt when she met Brónagh. And I was also relieved to see that I could share my supernatural feelings of destiny with her. This supposedly brutally blunt person gave me a reply that to me sums up the nature of true friendship: 'I feel like it's me that this is happening to, I'm that happy for ya! Really!'

I had never taken too much interest in all this talk about soulmates. The last thing I wanted to do when I was single was to be longing for a hypothetical relationship and let that longing ruin the good times I was having as a grown-up independent person. So I did not think about getting married or having children. I never felt this pang of envy when looking at other couples. I never thought about finding my better half – my *'media naranja'* ('other half of an orange'), as they say in Spanish. In the background, however, my mind was busy putting together the pieces of who I really am, and getting a clear idea of what is a real partner and what is a real relationship to me. I didn't put it into words, and certainly not images, but I knew what I wanted. I knew that I would never again settle for anything less, and I didn't care if it meant that I hadn't slept with a woman in three years.

Today I have an eerie certitude that this love that Katyna and I share goes beyond this world and that even death will not part us. I feel that I had been getting ready to meet her, and when I did I recognised her as if I'd always known who she would be. I had met others through my brain and my subconscious. I was now meeting her with my soul, and my whole self was shifting to a higher, better level as a result of this ray of pure love that was coming my way. I have fallen in love before, and I have gone through the phase of euphoria at the start of a relationship. But this time I felt something different, a truer, calmer type of happiness. I think it's called bliss.

We've now been together for six months, and we are preparing to come to Dublin to attend Orla and Brónagh's wedding. My eyes water with emotion every time I think about that day: the nerves, the look on Orla's face, and her and Brónagh's smiles when they say 'I do.'

Their wedding will be followed by Pride weekend, and yet another monster meetup where the Running Amach women take over an entire venue. I can't wait to see everyone again!

In its first seven months of existence, the Barcelona L Friends group has grown from five to seventy women and, although it doesn't nearly compare with the fast and ever-expanding success of Running Amach, we have a wonderful group of very diverse women, who all seem to be delighted to have found a community. For the first time in my life, I catch myself thinking about my own wedding, and I am very grateful that the law in Spain allows it. I am hopeful that France's new president will make it possible in my home country, and I can't wait to see it happen in Ireland – hopefully it will come with other invitations to other beautiful weddings!

On this note, I would like to thank the Running Amachs of the world for allowing Orla and I – and a lot of other women, I hope – to meet the other halves of their oranges, which possibly may have led to many marriages. Now I have to remember to pack tissues for the Dublin trip.

Cécile – 'Joan of Running Amach'

The Red Tartan Dress

My sister Jane (name changed) was in hospital for over three years due to having contracted TB in her hip. Her homecoming was imminent, and there was great excitement in our house when my parents arrived home and laid out on the back of a dining-room chair the red tartan dress.

I will never forget the feeling I had at the sight of that dress. I was green with envy! I was only eight years old and I had always felt inside that I should have been a girl. I thought that dress would look great on me. At the first opportunity, I intended to wear it, but I couldn't let anyone see me doing it. I might have been only eight years old, but somehow I knew not to give my secret away to anyone for fear of being declared insane. Not that I knew the term 'insane', but I felt I had to protect myself.

One day, my mother went to the shops, and I made for the dining room, my nerves trembling with excitement and fear all at once. I quickly got out of my boys' clothes, slipped the dress over my head and pulled it down over my body. It fitted me perfectly – well, I thought so anyway. I wanted to see the dress on me, but the only full-length mirror in the house was in my parents' bedroom. I was going to have to run the gauntlet of possibly running into my younger brothers, but I just had to see it.

I ran upstairs and into my parents' bedroom. I could see for myself just how pretty the dress looked on me. I thought it really should be mine. I stayed for as long as I dared, admiring myself and thinking how comfortable I felt wearing this beautiful tartan dress. A few minutes later, I ran back downstairs and changed back into my boys' clothes. I laid out the dress just as it had been. I can still to this day feel the sadness of having to leave the dress there and walk out of the room as if nothing had happened. That was the beginning of my conscious decision to dress in female clothes whenever I got the opportunity, because after all, 'I am a girl. But it's my secret!'

I am the eldest of a large Irish family. Dressing in female clothing was never easy, as all but one of my siblings were boys. But needs must, and I kept doing it whenever I could. This involved wearing my sister's clothes or my mum's. It mattered little that my mum's clothes didn't fit me; I just felt right in those garments.

As I got older, I eventually got a room to myself facing the road, so I could see the activity of people walking and children playing out my window. I would look at the girls playing and would long to be out there with them, one of the girls. It would break my heart that I couldn't do the girlie things they were doing; often I would lie on my bed and cry. I would ask God, 'Please let me be a girl when I wake up in the morning.' It never did happen, though!

Somehow I knew I must keep my secret to myself and, as I grew into my teens, I was even more acutely aware of having to maintain my secret. To ensure no one found me out, I would be as good as the next guy, or as tough as I needed to be in order to hold my own with the boys.

Then one day, the inevitable happened. I was probably about nineteen. My mum had been out shopping, and I was dressed as a girl while I had the house to myself. I heard the sound of the hall door opening and sheer panic ensued as I frantically tried to get out of the clothes I was wearing. At the same time I could hear her calling me, and I heard her approaching my room. The more I tried to undress the less I was able to, and I thought I would dive under the bed and hope she wouldn't notice. What was I thinking? Of course she could see the hem of my skirt sticking out from under the bed! What's more, she probably heard me getting under it, anyway. I can still hear her voice now.

'Get out from there. Now! What is going on?'

With a knot in the pit of my stomach, I sheepishly crept out from under the bed, wanting the ground to swallow me up. Mum stood there in total shock and said, 'Wait till your father comes home!' With that, she walked out of the room. Now, you would think that a nineteen-year-old would be able to stand up for themselves but I knew that if my mother couldn't understand, there was no possibility of my father being able to, and he a construction worker! I was in big trouble.

In those days, a nineteen-year-old was probably similar to a fifteen-year-old today. I got quite a bashing from my father when he did come home. I just took it. Somehow I was being punished for being me. A girl who was born with the body of a boy – how cruel is that, I ask? What sort of god gets his kicks from doing such things to a person? Why didn't he match my body with my brain?

These questions went on in my head for many years. At least one can see a person with a physical disability, but nobody saw me with any disability because it's not visible. All I ever wanted was to be the girl I could feel inside and be 'normal' – oh that dreaded word! Well, I did try to be a 'normal' guy. My mum's way of dealing with this matter was to haul me off to see a priest, a Jesuit in Gardiner Street who heard my confession. For fuck's sake, what was my sin?

Later, I met and fell in love with a beautiful woman. We eventually married and had three children. I didn't tell her about my secret for fear she would reject me. I continued to 'dress' whenever possible, which was usually when she was out at something and I knew I would have a few hours to be 'Claire'. I even took some photos of myself, which eventually caused me a lot of grief. I must have been careless because one day she found the photos and there was great shock. My wife thought I was having an affair with some girl who I even took home to our house. She never recognised that the girl in the photos was me.

It became the lesser of evils to explain to her that the woman in the photos was, in fact, me. I then had to explain to her exactly what I am, which, in those days, was known as transsexual, a term I have always disliked. There were lots of tears that lasted for weeks.

I decided then to seek professional help. I went to London to see a specialist, who confirmed that I am transgender. There was no such professional in Ireland at the time; that trip became my only option. I was able to commence hormone treatment and soon could feel the benefits. My breasts began to grow, and my hair became softer, and my skin too. I was elated! My specialist made it clear that my wife and I must divorce in order to continue the path to sex reassignment surgery. This was something neither of us wanted to do at the time, and so everything went on the long finger. At least I was officially recognised as a transgender woman. Yippee! I had to return to London every three months for a prescription, which I thought was crazy, so I asked the specialist if he could recommend someone in Dublin who might issue the prescription. After some consideration, he gave me the name of a doctor in St Patrick's Hospital.

I will never forget my first appointment with him. He had no idea how to deal with me. It was I who had to give him the details of my prescription, which he duly followed. Finally I had what I needed without having to make the expensive trip to London. I'll never forget the first day I presented the prescription to the pharmacist in Foley's Pharmacy on Baggot Street. He looked at me as if I had ten heads. He said something about there being some mistake, and I responded by telling him there was no mistake. I explained to him that I am a transgender woman and required the hormones. He told me to leave it with him; he needed to contact the doctor, and I should call back later that day. Hello, Ireland of the 1980s!

I co-founded a trans group in the late 70s/early 80s, and created a dedicated telephone line based out of my office. I had my own business in those days. My co-founder and I set about finding a place where we could have a meetup once a week. That venue became a top-floor room in the Parliament Inn, now the Turk's Head. We advertised meetings in *In Dublin* magazine, gave the phone number (a landline) and asked people to contact us only on Thursdays. While we got constant calls between 6 p.m. and 8 p.m. on Thursdays, there were also many calls outside of those hours.

Eventually, RTÉ got to know what we were doing, and a well-known presenter, Áine O'Connor (now deceased), came to the 'club' and did a few interviews (backs to camera), while her then boyfriend, actor Gabriel Byrne, sat at the bar drinking a pint or two. In fact, he came with her more than once to the meetup. Later, I was asked by RTÉ to do a magazine programme called *Summerhouse*, again with Áine O'Connor as the anchor.

Following on from that, Pat Kenny invited two transvestites, a wife of one of them, and me to appear on his morning radio show. All of this took place in the 1980s, which I would contend was the beginning of letting the Irish public know that people like us (transgender) exist in this country. *The Late Late Show* wanted in on the act too, and I came under enormous pressure to appear on it, but I wasn't ready to do that, as I was thinking of my family and trying to protect them from the possible fallout. Yes, I am a coward! As a compromise, I got an actor who is also a transvestite to appear on the show, and the piece was well received. I was present in the audience. I remember, though, the senior researcher, Colman Hutchinson, visiting me several times at my office and taking me to lunch with a view to convincing me to appear on the show. He would say things like you are the ideal person etc. for the show. When that failed, they had Gay Byrne's PA call me on a number of occasions, but I was resolute in my decision not to appear on it. Colman Hutchinson later became the director of the UK's *Who Wants to Be a Millionaire?*

We in the trans community have come a very long way since those pioneering days and, of course, today we have Transgender Equality Network Ireland (TENI) doing invaluable work for the trans community in Ireland.

I never did divorce, though we separated twelve years ago, and I never did go through with the sex reassignment surgery, but I have found a peace in my life in recent years, much of it due to the existence of that wonderful social networking site, Running Amach. So sincere thanks to all those wonderful women, who accept me as I am.

Claire Farrell

The Sixties and Me

In the late 1960s, Ireland was changing, but change occurred more slowly outside the major cities. I was brought up in Dundalk, County Louth, which was one of the largest rural towns at the time. I could see that young people were adopting modern dress and listening to popular music, as I did myself, and going to 'hops' and to dances where a growing number of showbands were playing. But underneath it all, I felt a conflict within me from the psychological burden of a Catholic Church mentality, which dominated Irish culture, politics, education and attitudes to sex and sexuality.

As a child growing up in the 1950s, the Church frightened the life out of me, preaching fire and brimstone from the pulpit, conveying the message to me that the Roman Catholic religion was the only true word of God, that the Pope was his represent-ative on earth, and anyone outside of this belief was condemned to hell. Hell was drummed into me as a terrible place to which I would go if I didn't follow, strictly, the teachings of the Church. I remember looking through the gates of a house at the end of our street, where strange people called Protestants lived, to see what people condemned to hell looked like.

What kind of message was I getting about sex and sexuality during my childhood? Well, mainly that the sexual act was a terrible sin, and very dirty, unless it was conducted between a married couple purely for procreation. Everything outside of that was taboo. This whole line of thinking followed me through the education system and was silently subscribed to by my parents. Sex was never discussed with me at home, except when my mother told me of the physical changes that would happen to me when I reached puberty. I went to two secondary schools, one in Dundalk, and then to a boarding school when I was fifteen. I don't remember any of the formal sex education, if any, that I received in the first of these schools. But in the boarding school I remember a nun telling us that if we were ever sitting on a boy's knee, we were to put a phonebook on his knee first, just in case!

I remember a priest being called in to tell us the mechanics of the sexual act between a man and a woman, and we all had to go individually into a room with him to be told. I remember feeling very uncomfortable about it at the time. If we wanted to get any enlightenment from our school library, we could forget it. The library consisted of books on Catholic theology, the classics like Dickens etc., some reference books on subjects we were studying, and little else. As I was taking physiology at one stage, I looked at the reference book on the subject. The pages of the whole chapter on the reproductive system had been physically torn from the book. Our textbook on the topic didn't suffer the same indignity; it merely stopped at the knee and started again at the belly button, leaving the unmentionable parts out altogether.

I was an only child, which was somewhat unusual at that time, as contraception was banned, and most of the families I knew had five-plus children. One family had 21! My mother lost twins when I was around four years old, and lost her womb as a result. My parents were very conscientious and caring parents, and I loved them dearly. I would describe them in three ways: first and foremost they were good parents to me, steeped in the Catholic tradition of family life, with high expectations for their only child. Second, I would describe them as pillars of the community. They were very outgoing, and my father specifically would be asked to MC many social events. They were involved in charitable work and also in the establishment and running of many social and sports activities. They were good singers and entertainers, and we had many good sessions in our house. And last but not least, politically they were Irish Republicans, and there were many discussions on Civil War politics at home. Like everything else they undertook, they put their heart and soul into their politics. Part of my mother's family came from the North, and we had many 'uncles' staying in our house, with the instruction that I was to tell no one because 'You don't want Mammy and Daddy to go to jail now, do you?' Absolutely not! So I kept mum and used to accompany my father as he drove them out to the border area at night, when they left our house. I have always held deep admiration for my parents for standing up for their political convictions.

At thirteen years of age, an event occurred which was to change my whole way of thinking. As I have already indicated, I had led a very sheltered life and was very naive, as were a lot of my friends in those days. I believed that Eve was a temptress because she actually stole an apple from a tree and tried to get Adam to eat it. It wasn't till later that I realised it was more to do with the pair on the ground than the apple on the tree. I also took to heart this extract about animals from the catechism: 'Animals are God's creatures. He surrounds them with his providential care. By their mere existence they bless Him and give Him glory. Thus, men owe them kindness.' Even though the Church said animals had no soul.

I also still believed in St Francis, Santa Claus, the Christmas Fairy and the Catholic Church. To say I was fanatical about the care of animals was putting it mildly. I hated cruelty to animals and as a child often 'rescued' animals when they didn't need it. But, when myself, my cousin who stayed with us at weekends, and a bunch of my friends were offered five old Irish pounds each to go out to the coursing club to make sandwiches for the lunch for the weekend, we all jumped at it. Five pounds was a lot of money in those days.

Of course, I had no idea what coursing was. After we had finished the lunch on the Saturday, which was the first day of the meet, we asked if we could go and watch the coursing and were given permission to do so. I remember walking up the stairs to the opening of the stand where it opened on to the coursing field. Halfway up the stairs we heard this almighty screech, which appeared to us as if a child was in extreme pain. We ran all the way up to the opening and were met with a sight which will stay with me forever. Two greyhounds were tearing a hare apart. One dog had the hare's back end in its mouth, the other had its face, and they were pulling it in opposite directions. The hare was screaming in pain. I felt as if a rock had gone through my heart. The crowd were cheering and clapping. I looked around and saw numerous dog collars; they weren't on the dogs.

It was at that moment that I realised that the human animal was the most flawed of all, capable of great cruelty. I still can't understand how people can get enjoyment from a so-called sport that inflicts pain and stress on another living thing. I was very distressed by the time I got home, not only at the cruelty involved but also at the amount of priests I saw cheering and clapping at the spectacle. I thought, 'Where is the teaching of the catechism now, "Thus men owe them kindness", when their own priests are breaking it?' I refused to go back the next day and was grounded.

During that Sunday in my bedroom alone I resolved to read every book I could find that was banned. Censorship was very strict but, like everything else, there were ways and means. I was the book reader in the family. I devoured a book a day. I got hold of books on the Vatican finances and the life and history of the popes. I learned that some of the Vatican finances had been invested in projects of a nefarious sexual nature and that some of the popes had been openly gay. I realised that it was a case of 'Do as I say not as I do', so I gave up the Catholic Church and organised religion, although I was still stuck in a Catholic education system.

I questioned everything. When I found out that it was the sexual act between Adam and Eve that was the forbidden fruit, I asked my mother why Eve was getting all the blame when Adam participated as well. I also asked her one day when we were both in the Redemptorist chapel what was happening at the side altar. She said a woman was getting 'churched', as she and her husband had just had a baby. She said 'churched' meant getting cleansed. I told her I thought that this was a bit rich, as the woman was doing everything that the Catholic Church said was right and why wasn't her husband getting churched as well? I was only fourteen at the time, and I think my constant questioning was getting on my mother's nerves. Her stock answer to everything was that I was too complicated and thought too deeply. But neither she nor I realised just how complicated I was to be become.

I wish I could say that mentally freeing myself from the yoke of Catholicism made my life easier, but then sex and sexuality reared its ugly head. I tried really hard to be like everyone else. I had my hair long, wore all the latest fashion in clothing, went with my friends to hops, was very active in the community and had boyfriends. The one problem was that I could never connect with the lads on any kind of a physical or sexual basis and found myself more sexually attracted to women. I read about homosexuality, specifically about Sappho and the island of Lesbos. I then looked for biblical references and found Leviticus 20.13: 'If there is a man who lies with a man as those who lie with a woman, both of them committed a detestable act, and they shall surely be put to death.' Although it referred to men only, I got the message: KILL ALL QUEERS! I looked further at Leviticus and discovered that it also said you were only to use a certain type of cloth and also kill your child if he disobeys you and other things like this, and so I decided that it was written by a man or men with all the prejudices of their own time and history.

I decided to ask my mother about homosexuality. She went into a big rant against it, naming a young man who was arrested by the Gardaí. He was caught with another man down the demesne, engaging in what she described as a filthy, dirty act. The young man had been put in jail. Being an active homosexual was illegal at the time. She said she knew his mother and that the woman was totally devastated. I got the message loud and clear and realised I would never be able to tell anyone about how I felt.

I was miserable in boarding school and didn't fit in at all. Some of the girls in the school said that lesbians looked like men. I didn't look like a man, but felt like a lesbian and was totally confused. The only consolation I had was that the gym teacher looked like the stereotype of a lesbian that I was given. She may not have been, but I convinced myself she was and so I didn't feel I was the only one. I had crushes on a number of girls but was afraid to act on them in case I was jailed.

My life was full of fear in that respect. However, leaving school was an even worse time for me. I didn't do well academically because I felt so miserable. I got a job I hated and couldn't find another young woman in Dundalk who I felt I could relate to sexually. I asked my parents if I could get a motorbike and be a rocker, thinking to myself that this might attract other women who felt like me. They said no daughter of theirs was going to ride around Dundalk on a motorbike. So we compromised on me being a mod if I saved up and bought a scooter myself, which I did. But even riding around on a scooter got me nowhere. I realised that I could never be the daughter my parents wanted: I would never produce children – sperm donation wasn't even discussed in that era. They would never be grandparents, and I wondered what use was there in me living any longer. I felt I was living my parents' life, not mine.

I had read about suicide and asked my dad why I rarely heard of any Irish person committing it. He told me that the Catholic Church believed that taking one's own life was a sin. Therefore, anyone doing so couldn't be buried in consecrated ground. This proved a statistical problem, as the graveyards were all consecrated, and there were no crematoria at the time. As a result, most suicides would be termed 'accidental deaths' so that the authorities wouldn't be left with a headache.

One day, while my parents were out, I put on the gas oven in the kitchen, unlit, and decided to end it all. My head was so melted, and I wasn't thinking straight, literally. But karma intervened, and someone knocked on the front door. By the time they had gone, I was feeling a bit more rational and decided I had another option: to emigrate to England and live my own life.

I told my parents I wanted to emigrate. This they took very badly, but I said that there was no practical or professional training here for the profession I wanted to get into, and England offered me the best opportunity. I never told them or anyone else the second reason. They said I could go with their blessing if I had a job to go to and a place to stay. The thing that kept me sane through all this was these lines from a song which I hummed constantly in my head: 'We Gotta Get Out of this Place'.

By the end of the summer of 1968 I had obtained a job in London, a place to stay, and I knew a place where I could go to meet other lesbians. At Dún Laoghaire, as I was about to embark, my father and mother started to cry. They saw it as a failure on their part that their only child was emigrating to England. I felt really guilty about hurting them, but deep inside I felt a sense of freedom.

In December 1968, as I was on the King's Road in Chelsea going down the steep stairway of the Gateways lesbian club, I realised that I had come home sexually and that coming to the 'auld enemy' had saved my life.

Lavender Jane

Who Am I?

My name is Margaret O'Donoghue. I'm Kerry-born and bred, and I am soon to be 34.

I am labelled a lesbian or bisexual, and most days wearing my persona of being an 'everyday Joe Soap' works. But on many days it hasn't.

What is life like for me?

My life, I feel, is cushioned. I made a choice some years back to act only on my attraction to women, as it is the stronger. So I surrounded myself with people who identify as having an attraction to the same sex. Friends I have known for many years or people who are understanding or sympathetic.

I have felt at times wrongly labelled, tolerated and not relevant. As a result of these prejudices from within myself, and society, I have experienced feelings of isolation, depression and not belonging anywhere. Therefore, I have decided to create a place for myself by being myself. I am a member of society whether it wants me or not!

I am one of the lucky ones. Thankfully, I told my mother of my sexuality a few years before she passed away. It was a struggle for her also. She thought it could negatively affect my life and that of my daughter. I have met many people with different backgrounds, beliefs, families, ages, etc. who do not feel safe enough, or do not feel that they have the support to tell their loved ones they are attracted to their own sex. The following memory is a moment in my life that has had a profound impact on me, and I think it will remain one of my strongest memories throughout my life.

Shortly after my daughter turned eight, I was preparing the evening meal while she sat directly behind me at the kitchen table doing her homework. Suddenly, I heard a 'Muuum'. I knew from experience that when the 'mum' is drawn out in that way, she has a serious question to ask. I turned around to face her.

'Yesss,' I said, in the same drawn-out manner, afraid of the question that was inevitably to come. When it did come, I wanted to run. Instead, I explained that a lesbian was a woman in love with another woman. I turned back to my cooking, relieved that I hadn't chickened out or changed the subject. Silently, I was hoping that that would be the end of it. However, after what felt like seconds, and while I was still getting my head around what had just occurred, there came a second long, drawn-out 'Mummm'.

Then came the second question, put so curiously and with such innocence.

'Are you a lesbian?'

'Oh God, I can't!' I thought. I felt EVERYTHING in those few seconds. I wanted to run, but I had to answer.

'Yes.'

Very quietly she just said, 'Oh!' Then she went back to her homework.

Relieved, I turned back to my sauce.

I am Margaret O'Donoghue. I am a mother, I am a lesbian and my daughter is just about to turn twelve.

Margaret O'Donoghue

Wicklow Street

'Hello, my name is Kate, and I am a lesbian.'

That is how we introduced ourselves at the coming-out group in Wicklow Street in 1985. Saying this saved us.

I only realised years later when I had to save myself again that this is how people introduced themselves at rehab meetings: 'Hello my name is ... and I am a ...'

You might think saving ourselves is a bit strong, but that's how it felt.

By the time I said it, I was 25 years old. Up to a few weeks earlier, I thought I was the only lesbian in Dublin. Apart from Nell McCafferty, that is, of whom, every time she came on TV, someone said, 'There's that lesbian, Nell McCafferty!'

Anyway, the coming-out meeting was held on the top floor of a six-storied house in Wicklow Street. There was a massage parlour on the fourth floor, with a peephole in the door. A blonde woman opened it every so often when she mistook one of us coming up the stairs for clients.

At the meeting we sat in a circle, usually about fifteen of us on big, comfortable couches. We started by introducing ourselves. My nerves were shattered the first week. Not knowing what to expect, I hardly said a word. But I do remember looking at the girls around me and thinking that they were just like all my other friends. They were chatty, friendly and having a laugh.

Maybe I could live this kind of life after all? Little did I know how soon I'd actually be proud to be a lesbian.

After we introduced ourselves, we each gave a brief explanation of why we were there. Mostly our stories were the same: the isolation, the shame and the sheer hopelessness. As the weeks went by, we could feel ourselves getting stronger and happier. At last we belonged somewhere, with people who understood us and had the same experiences. I remember thinking, 'Now I can start to live, now I have a life, and now I fit in. Thank God I found this out now and not when I'm 80!'

The meetings went on for about two hours, and then we would go up the road to JJ Smyth's, a women-only disco. In fact, the only women's disco in Ireland. It was upstairs, a long room that held about a hundred people. At one end there was a dancefloor and a DJ, and at the opposite end was a bar. In between were seats and tables and an aisle down the centre, through which you had to walk down to get to the dancefloor.

The first time I walked down to the dancefloor, I had been asked to dance. This woman came over to our table and looked at me. She then nodded towards the dancefloor. It was a real Robert De Niro moment of 'You lookin' at me?' To my delight, she was. So I shyly obeyed. It felt really odd to be so close to a woman I had only met seconds before, with her cheek at my ear and her hands around my waist. We danced to Patti LaBelle and Michael McDonald's 'On My Own'. I knew there and then that this was going to be part of my future.

I lived every week to go to Wicklow Street. I had two pairs of good jeans that I adored, one black and one navy, Bananarama-style. I alternated them every week. Suddenly, I was experiencing all the things my straight friends had been enjoying since their early teens – the excitement of getting ready and having new clothes. Better late than never, I thought. Our group did all the gay marches, the women's weekends, the camping holidays and every feminist meeting in Dublin. We had a ball!

Within months, I had fallen in love with a woman whom I would end up spending ten years with. I met the apple of my eye in Wicklow Street. She arrived on a Kawasaki 100 and chained it to a pole outside the door. She said afterwards it was to stop someone throwing it into the skip. She wore a green cardigan and pale-green checked jeans, and she had a wicked sense of humour.

That night, the group decided that instead of going to the pub we would play Scrabble on the floor. The apple of my eye lay on her tummy opposite me with her heels in the air. She clicked them loudly when she thought of a long word. I silently said to myself, 'There is a God. I am going to ask her to dance later.' We were invited to a party in Harrington Street where we both sat on the steps outside. Joan Armatrading's 'Love and Affection' was playing inside, and she asked me to dance.

Kate

Woman by Nature, Confused by Birth

In the swinging sixties in the back bedroom of a working-class house in west Dublin, a girl was born, but a boy was celebrated. I was physically a boy but a girl inside.

Imagine a child living a nightmare unable to understand the nature of his or her birth: the silent screams, the prayers every night, a hope for a miracle and feeling totally alone within a huge family. Imagine that same child in a schoolyard full of happy children, skipping and laughing without a care in the world.

I never experienced a happy childhood, not because of being poor or because of the holes in the soles of my shoes and not because of bad parents. I was unhappy within the world that I was forced to live in, with a gender that was alien to the one I saw myself as. I was not a boy, I was a girl.

I was very scared and introverted as a child. To cope with this feeling of being someone else and of being too scared to tell anyone, I went into my dream world, my haven, a place where I was safe, but I had to awaken sometimes and come back to the real world, my scary real world where only panic and confusion awaited me.

I just drifted along in school. I could not learn to read or write. I was labelled a troublemaker by the teachers. I was beaten almost every day by the teacher for not trying hard enough to learn. In the schoolyard, I was bullied and beaten by the boys, because I would not get involved with their playground games. At break times I used to hide in the toilets and only come out when the bell rang to line up for class again. Because of this I was slagged and derided by the boys who called me 'weirdo' and 'queer maggot'. Had I been in a mixed school, perhaps my young years might have been a bit easier.

Every day when I left my house, I was entering my nightmare. Living with a gender confusion that was to bring me to the brink of darkness and to the edge of life itself. My soul ached for peace. My tears ran dry, and all hope disappeared. My only thoughts were of dying.

What exactly is gender? When do you become male or female? It took me a lot of time and heartache to find my own self-respect. I knew I had to respect myself before I could expect anyone else to accept me. Who had the right to impose a gender identity upon me?

As a child born with a condition of being a female within a male body, how could I understand my situation or foretell the hell that was to lie ahead of me in my quest for acceptance from a society that preferred to laugh at me than to listen to me? It was up to one person, myself, to find a way.

I did not choose my path to be born the way I was; this is something beyond anyone's control. No blood test or X-ray could help anyone see my true nature of being female. Fate had dealt me a cruel blow early on, as at some point in the early stages of our development we each become either female or male. For some of us, our bodies develop in the opposite way physically to our brain gender; female brain in a male body in my case. I wish people could realise that we are not the sum of our body parts and that the physical body that assumes to hold a matching female or male identity does not always match one's true gender. I am a true soul and certain of my female identity. No amount of misunderstanding, pills or bullying will change or direct me from my true nature of being a woman.

Whether you identify me as having been born with a gender identity disorder or as transgender, the fact remains that I did not fit into what was assigned to me at birth. The only sex I ever identified as was and is female. I did not have a choice within the womb to dictate the nature of my birth or the formation of my body. Nature sometimes has a cruel way to preserve human life at all cost, and this is why I suppose some people are born with conditions that are still, even in these days of modern medicine or science, not fully explainable. I can only speak of my own very unhappy childhood, living with the effect of my birth and being assigned the wrong gender.

What harm did I do in pursuing my true gender and going ahead with full gender reassignment to live both physically and socially as a female? What right has society to regard me in any other way than simply as a woman? If one believes in the soul and that the body is only a carriage for that soul throughout a natural lifespan, and we are supposed to honour our natural lifespan, then am I not being true to my soul in deciding to live the rest of my natural life as a woman? Surely to take my own life would have been a waste and caused the most harm to myself and my family. Do I not have a right to find love and to have a family? Would it not be a fair justice to me and others if society was not so preoccupied with gender and pathology or tags? Because of my birth and my gender identity, my life in my younger years was hell on earth. It nearly killed me. It turned me into a liar and an introverted child who gave out all the wrong vibes. I was crying deeply inside, and it got to the stage that I had no more tears or emotions left for anyone or anything.

I never felt right within the body that I was carrying through life with me, my fragile little life that was hanging by a thread. I never fitted into the role that was thrust upon me by doctors, my parents and society. At five years of age, I discovered I was different from other girls, even though I felt right in their world. In discovering this difference, my world came crashing down. I had only ever thought of myself as being the same as other little girls. I went into a secret world of my own, a fantasy one where 'Lynda' was perfect. I had my secret doll's house, my dolls, my lovely dresses and all the girlie things that were denied me in reality.

I used to hear the careless whispers of others who would say things like, 'That child is very pale', 'Something is not right about that child', or 'You cannot trust a child like that.' How was anyone to know the truth? No one ever imagined that I was a girl – no one!

At eight, I approached a local priest and told him in confession how I felt, in the best way a child could. His response was to pull me by the ear into the back room and give me a dressing down, telling me that I can't go around telling people I am a girl. He said, 'You will be locked up. Pray and ask God for forgiveness and thank Him for the body that you have.' I left that church wanting to die. That day was to be my first suicide attempt.

I walked out on to the road wanting to be hit by a car, hoping that I would wake up and realise it was all a dream. My life remained intact. No car hit me. All I got was abuse from drivers. 'Get off the road, you bleeding idiot!'

I believed that I was doomed to be stuck in a body that was killing my very soul and my wish to live. I was very sad in a way that was indescribable for me. I left school at eleven years of age, unable to read or write. No one in social services cared, and I was forgotten. I drifted around, hiding in the fields or down by the river day after day. Was I ever going to be happy? Was I ever going to be free of this agony? I could not imagine living like this forever. Death was always on my mind. I imagined that if I just dropped into the water, it would be so easy to end my pain. The fight and hope within me were all but gone.

In my pre-teenage years, I attempted suicide for the second time. I took an overdose of tablets I found in the house and drank motor oil with them. Yes, motor oil! I wanted to make sure I was successful this time. It wasn't to be, however. I threw up almost immediately, and all the tablets and diesel and everything else came up. I guess life was not done with me yet. I was only twelve years old. It was summertime, but I had only darkness within me. I drifted along again. I played the part that society had thrust upon me. I accepted that I was never going to be happy or free to be the real me.

When I was fourteen, I remember being jealous of all the girls getting ready and dressed up in their pretty frocks and make-up. I envied them and felt so lonely. Death was the only way I could see back then of escaping the nightmare of my life and finding the peace I so longed for with my sweet Lord. I hadn't believed in the Church for a long time, but I did believe in God. I knew that He would understand and forgive me for not wanting this life of hell I was living. I thought all was lost until I began hanging around the flats on Dorset Street. I always stood at the wall in silence. The boys and girls had stopped hitting me and jeering me by then. They used to say, 'Aww, it's just the weirdo', and they would leave me there in my lonely spot. Then something happened that was to be the start of the rest of my life. The beginning of the truth of Lynda.

This girl approached me, and all the other girls were giggling, urging her over to me. As she came near me, she looked like an angel. Honestly, I could see this light around her! It seemed to take ages for her to approach me. What she said was to blow my mind. A burst of emotions rushed through my body, to my very soul. Little did I realise this moment was to be the most important one in my life.

'I know they call you a weirdo, but I don't think you are,' Carmel said. 'You are very good-looking. Do you want to be my boyfriend?'

Wow, wow, wow! From that moment, I knew we were going to be together forever.

In response, I grabbed her and brought her across the yard. I just yelled out, 'I can't! I can't be your boyfriend! I am a girl. Please, please do not tell anyone or I will be killed. I don't know why I feel this way. Please don't tell anyone!'

For some incredible reason, it was the first time in my life that I could tell someone my truth. She stalled for a moment and then said, 'Well, why don't we go out together and try it, and if you feel that way I will help you.' Believe me, she was an incredible girl for her age. She was also just fourteen.

We hung out together for about a year and were very happy. It was not a burden for me to play the role of boyfriend with Carmel. Then one day, suddenly, she disappeared out of my life. She no longer hung around the flats. I was distraught. I didn't know where she lived, and there were no mobiles or Facebook in those days. So I drifted back into my surreal world, my place where life hung by a thread. I thought I had found my hope, my love, my acceptance, my life and my perfect partner. I was sixteen, and I was still alive. Well, sort of.

One day I was walking down Dorset Street towards the flats where we used to hang out. I was looking for Carmel; day after day I was looking for her, but I had had no luck. I ached for her. That day, as I was walking up North Circular Road, there she was! Some force had directed me to her. She had grown up and was even more beautiful. She looked at me, and I looked at her for what felt like forever. The world stood still and quiet, then I let out a shout, 'It's you! It's you!'

She started to walk towards me, saying nothing. Then she picked up pace, and we ran into each other's arms. We vowed never to leave each other again. She told me she had been ill for a number of years and that is why I hadn't seen her until that day. We were both now seventeen. We kissed, hugged, cried, and she promised to help me. She was indeed a girl wise beyond her years.

We searched for answers to how I felt, and we could not find anything anywhere. There was no internet then. So it was in the gay section of the local library that we found some answers to explain in some way how I felt. It was all about 'transgender' and other terms I did not like. The only term I liked was 'female', nothing else. But I did learn about those who do identify as transgender, and this helped in some ways.

Carmel and I decided to stay together. We moved into a flat on the North Circular Road, where Lynda could be just that – Lynda. We did yearn for more from life, however. We wanted a house, a car and children. All the normal things a loving couple wants. Alas, we realised that that was not going to be easy in the world we lived in then. We decided to play the game of a straight couple. We got married and had three wonderful children. I could be Lynda sometimes, in private and on holidays. We decided that we would get our children educated first and through at least secondary school before my full and final transition.

But life was to throw an awful blow that would jeopardise our happy life together. Carmel, my true love and soulmate, was diagnosed with cancer. This battle was to last seven years, but her health never improved. I loved her so much! She loved me too. I had the most wonderful time in life with her. She was and will remain my true love. My soulmate. My everything! She gave me life, my children, and now eight wonderful grandchildren. My life is full with my children and grandchildren, but there will always be a void, a sadness and an emptiness without her. She passed away over fifteen years ago. Some day, we will be together again, walking with our son who is walking with her. I found the greatest love with her. I have been so lucky, and she has given me the strength to go on.

As she lay on the bed taking her last breaths, I promised her that I would live my natural lifespan and help others for as long as I could. We met so young. I lost her and found her again, only to lose her again physically. But her spirit keeps me going, for she is my guardian angel, sent from God to me for a while to get me where I am today, to give me courage to help others and to live a natural lifespan. Carmel gave me her whole life, the greatest love and all the lovely little people in my life. Had she walked out of my life when we were teenagers, I would have been so lonely and without direction.

My daughters are wonderful. They have accepted Lynda into their lives, not to replace Carmel in any way, for she is irreplaceable, but in order to see me happy and content. I'm a loving parent who is very much in their lives.

I have finally achieved my true gender, my lust for life, my wonderful community and my belief in myself that I am worthy of love. Some day my true love and I will walk again in peace and harmony.

My advice to those suffering what I have suffered is to never give up hope. In the end, you will achieve your true self. It has taken me a long time, along many rocky roads, but finally I am home. I have made it through the rain.

Every day I miss my soulmate, but she is guiding me along. I still have things to achieve in this world and a worthwhile life to live.

Dedicated to my wonderful true love, Carmel, RIP.
And to my son, Kevin Jason, RIP.
Also to my two wonderful daughters, Sinéad and Carola, who have embraced me without fear.

Lynda Sheridan

You and Me

As I sit here, smoking my Marlboro Lights, watching you make us coffee, I see your left breast revealing itself from your yellow towel robe. I remember the first time I touched you. I was so afraid and wet with excitement all at the same time. I had rehearsed it in my mind a hundred million times.

You hand me my cup and ask me how many slices of toast I want. Two. Just butter, no marmalade. I notice your hair needs a cut. You mouth the words, 'I love you', and then feed the dogs. I wonder how many different kinds of love there are. I can feel my heart hurt now.

I think of the first time we spent the whole weekend in bed, waking up and burying my face in your most beautiful, soft, rounded breasts. Every sense in my body is awoken. I will you to just slide down between my legs, suck me, taste me, and make love to me.

You're smiling at me. You ask me what I'm thinking. I put out my cigarette and say I'm going to have a shower. You catch my hand as I pass and kiss it. I smile.

Standing in the shower, I wash my hair, caress my breasts, watching the suds slide down the curves. I am still attractive, aren't I? I feel the heat of my tears falling down my face. Stepping out of the shower, I catch a glimpse of myself in the mirror, trying to remember the last time we showered together. I can't.

You kiss me on the mouth as you leave for work. 'Have a good day. I'll make dinner tonight,' you say. And so another day begins. I've stopped hoping that when you come home this evening, it will be any different than it has been for the last year. Every phone call, every conversation, every gesture … I used to wait for you to say that you had gone to the doctor about your libido, or that you had gone to a sex therapist, or that, even just one morning, you would wake up filled with an uncontrollable need to make love to me. But you have always been too busy or you forgot. So we stopped talking about it.

The dogs and I stand here in the doorway, watching you drive down the driveway. I mouth, 'I love you' as I close the front door and go to my designs. I know there won't be many more days like these. One day soon, the dogs and I won't be standing watching you drive down the driveway.

Gormla Hughes

You Deserve to Wake Up to Someone You Love

It was the early seventies, and I was like all the other seventeen-year-olds: I had a boyfriend, went dancing on the weekends, went to the pictures during the week, and spent endless hours with my 'girlfriends' in their houses, them talking about their boyfriends and me making all the right sounds, while staring lovingly into Anne's eyes as she banged on about this boy or that. You see, I was different, but I didn't want to be. I just wanted to fit in, do what was expected of me and get on with it. There was no such thing as gay rights in 1973. I was the youngest of eight children. My parents had been born in the first half of the twentieth century. They wouldn't understand.

What was I to do? Overcompensate! At eighteen I got engaged to Mike. A lovely, handsome and very patient young man. He was two years older than me. His mother had recently died, so he wanted to get married, pull his family (kid brothers and sister) together and start his own family.

Holy shit! How will I get around this?

I had never been with a man, boy or girl in my life. The thought filled me with dread. How the fuck was I going to get out of this? He was a lovely guy, and everyone liked him. He was respectful, thank God! That had helped me out of a few sticky moments. Still, I was not going to let everyone down and be the 'old maid' in the family. The one who was a bit strange. I was sure everybody was suspicious of me and could see me looking at girls.

God help me! I was sure I would eventually get used to the sex thing. And so far so good; I was being a good girl. Time moved forward, and it was getting closer to the time that we should be making preparations for the wedding. I must have looked like the most reluctant bride-to-be ever. There were days where I could feel my mother's eyes burning into my soul. I could feel her watching me with those beautiful grey-blue eyes of hers. I was sure she knew and disapproved of me. She often looked sad at those times.

During that summer, my best friend, who worked in the same factory as me, broke up with her boyfriend. This was the best news in the world to me, as he didn't treat her well. He was an asshole! I would have jumped through hoops for her. Why couldn't I get the same shivery feelings for Mike when he was with me? Why did I race to work early, so Anne and I could walk into work together? We would stop at the shop to buy our fags, and I would often get her chocolate. As I gave it to her, our fingers would touch, and I would almost go weak at the knees. Every night, I would feel sick for Mike as he got excited about our future plans, as we went flat-hunting, looking at flower shops and suits, dresses, etc. I had no enthusiasm for our impending life together.

What was I to do? Who could I talk to? There was no one else like me in the whole of Dublin. Maybe I could run away? It was all very fine and dandy feeling all weak at the knees about Anne but, fucking hell, she didn't even notice me! She was talking about getting back with the asshole. Bet he didn't tell her she was great or pretty or buy her chocolate ... who was I fooling? She would die if she knew how I felt about her! I couldn't bear to see the look of disgust in her eyes if she found out. The look I am sure I could see in my mother's eyes every time she looked at me.

Then, one summer's evening, Mam asked me not to make any plans for the following night. 'We can go for a walk; it's such lovely weather, and we never seem to spend time together any more.' As the youngest, I spent a lot of time with her as a kid. We both had a great love of books and reading and got on really well. Since I had started work, I hadn't been spending as much time with her. I missed our chats. She was a very clever woman, well read and funny. So it was agreed that we would go out after dinner the next evening. I was looking forward to it.

Wednesday evening we ate dinner in good-spirited conversation, Dad gently teasing Mam in his fashion and waiting for her usual quick and smart answers. He enjoyed their verbal jousting as much as I did. They were a great auld team and clearly loved each other. Then we started on our walk, and the conversation very quickly came around to my impending marriage – a little too quickly! I was no match for my mother. If she wanted to talk about something or get information out of you, you didn't stand a chance. Then came the bombshell.

'Mike is a nice boy and deserves better!'

My head snapped around. 'What?'

Calmly she repeated herself. 'He deserves better.'

'What, better than me?' I was hurt and angry. 'How could you? My own mother!'

She was very calm. 'I didn't say better than you. If you will only listen. I said "better", and so do you!'

'Me! What? How …'

'He deserves to wake up in the morning to someone who loves him,' she shouted, 'just as you deserve to wake up to someone you love, no matter who that person is! That's the problem with you young people, you all think you have the monopoly on life, that you invented everything. Back in the thirties, when I first came to Dublin, I had friends like you. People called them bohemians. They were the greatest bunch of boys and girls but had it hard because they were different. It doesn't matter who you love! What's important is that you learn to love yourself. I will still love you and so will your father. The rest of them, well, we may have a battle with them. They're not as open as me.'

I stood there, ashen-faced, with my mouth open, on that most beautiful of nights in early July 1973.

'My mother is saying she had friends like me back in the thirties!' I thought. 'I can't possibly get married to Mike and fuck up his life, and mine!'

Then she handed me a piece of paper with the name 'Bartley Dunne's' written on it – a famous gay pub, as I was soon to learn – and a phone number for a newly formed lesbian helpline. I nearly dropped dead on the spot.

Then she said, 'It all makes perfect sense to me. Now I know why you have no dress sense!'

I didn't know if I should run away or stay and hug her. But, as always, she knew exactly what to do. 'First, let's go get some chips for supper, and then I will help you with ways to word it when you tell Mike.'

God bless her! I could have made a huge mistake and, as she said, ruined two lives if I had gone ahead with trying to make everybody else happy.

When I did find my first girlfriend, Clare, both my father and my mother welcomed her into the family. They were very fond of her. While she and I saved to go to England in the eighties because there was no work here, they put us up and helped us out. We had our own room, just like anyone else in the family who was staying with them. I know Clare adored them both.

Forty years on, we are still good friends. Now when we meet up, we always drink a toast to 'The Mother!' Her name was Johanna.

Ailisha